JACK KEROUAC— OUTSIDE WRITING

A Pocket Biography

JACK KEROUAC — OUTSIDE WRITING

A Pocket Biography

R.J. Ellis

Prestige
an international publishing house
New Delhi Sydney

Published by
PRESTIGE BOOKS
3/28, East Patel Nagar
New Delhi 110 008
Ph: 9818755529

Associate Office
60/29-45, Parramatta Raod
Concord, NSW 2137
Australia

e-mail: prestigebooks@gmail.com
website: www.asiabookclub.com

ISBN 81-7851-043-X

Printed at Chaman Offset Press, New Delhi 110 002

Contents

Introduction

DEDICATED TO AMERICA, WHATEVER THAT IS (Jack Kerouac, *Visions of Cody*, 1959)

Jack Kerouac (1922-1969)—the writer and the man—is invested in so many layers of legend, sensationalism and myth, that, like the Beatles or Elvis, it is almost impossible to grasp hold of anything about him that is not shaped by his star status. Yet his celebrity did much to destroy him: he was a man who could not handle fame.

This short biography seeks to dig beneath the aura investing his election as 'King of the Beatniks' (*BS*, 4)[1] and to uncover the more complex reality of his life. Kerouac fitted uneasily into the coterie of writers emerging in mid-century America. To understand why, his status as a Beat writer and his media construction as 'King of the Beats' need to be placed beside a set of other influences: his French-Canadian Catholic origins in working-class Lowell, where he grew up; his intensive experiments in writing, as he sought to develop a 'spontaneous bop prosody' rooted in what he called 'deep form';[2] his striving for an authenticity that he knew was always eluding him; his passionate engagement with his society and its culture, within which his oscillating feelings about his milieu swung between love and mistrust; his admiration for some of the past masters of Modernism (particularly Dostoyevsky, Proust, Céline and Joyce); his ever-increasing doubts about his sexual identity; his long struggle with alcoholism and drugs; and his increasingly over-close relationship with his mother. Kerouac's writing constantly negotiates between these aspects of his identity, and the frequent conflicts between them.

Kerouac, as he composed *On the Road* at high speed over a twenty-day period in 1951, also launched out on an endlessly honest quest for authenticity: how exactly to convey his life and experience. What he immediately found was that authenticity was not just out there waiting to be seized. Rather, any such romantic quest was constantly frustrated by social constraints, pre-shaping 'meaning' so that it constantly has to be re-negotiated: never quite becoming pure, always stubbornly remaining adulterated. So, for Kerouac, authenticity inevitably remained elusive, even as he sought to transcribe it. The arrival of fame simply drove truth further off into the thickets, and with burning, even shaming, honesty he portrays how this happened in his later novels, such as *Big Sur* and *Satori in Paris*.

Perhaps fortunately then, given his inability to handle it, fame was slow to arrive. Instead, largely ignored in the late 1940s and early 1950s except by a coterie of writers—the Beats and those artists associated with them—and left largely unpublished except for his first, untypical novel, *The Town and the City*, Kerouac could concentrate on developing his art. For almost a full decade, roughly from 1948 to 1957, he was writing with enormous rapidity. Often he wrote large amounts on a daily basis, forging in the process a prose style that became extraordinarily versatile and quite different from any writing that preceded it.

Jack Kerouac's appearance on a commemorative postage stamp after his death indicates the scale of the fame he could not satisfactorily handle.

This style has many influences including Thomas Wolfe, Ernest Hemingway, William Faulkner, James Joyce, Walt Whitman, Herman Melville, and William Shakespeare alongside Dostoyevsky, Proust, Céline and Joyce. Kerouac was also much influenced by the writing of his friends, particularly Neal Cassady, William Burroughs and Allen Ginsberg. But simply listing all these names makes apparent how inevitable it was that such a diverse range of influences would lead Kerouac in new artistic directions. That these directions turned out to be so startling resulted from the way Kerouac additionally drew upon a long list of popular cultural influences—cartoons, comic books, journalism, films (particularly B-movies), crime writing, thrillers and other pulp writing, not to mention his deep interest in Chinese and Japanese poetry, Buddhist writing, Gnosticism and environmentalism. He omnivorously brought together the popular and the 'literary', with a new kind of open-mindedness about how these could fit together and what could result.

In order to understand how Kerouac's writing developed, it is first necessary to establish some idea of his fiction's order-of-writing. Yet determining this order is not easy: often Kerouac worked on several pieces of writing simultaneously, so creating a complex, overlapping sequence. For example, whilst working on a long series of revisions to *On the Road* in the 1950s, Kerouac also put the finishing touches to *The Town and the City* and wrote *Visions of Cody*, *Doctor Sax*, *Maggie Cassidy*, *The Subterraneans*, *Visions of Gerard*, *Tristessa*, plus a number of poetry sequences which he called his *Books of Blues*—and more besides.

Furthermore, the order in which Kerouac wrote his books does not match the order in which they were published (see Appendix B.i). This mismatch results from the fact that Kerouac's relationship with the American publishing industry was far from easy. Publishers for the most part failed to grasp what he was trying to do. Kerouac, in return, felt that almost all of the editing his publishers insisted upon damaged his novels. This conviction set in early, after *The Town and the City* was poorly reviewed. Kerouac blamed this rejection on the large-scale editing he had been asked to carry out.

This feeling became almost an obsession when his editor reacted poorly to the presentation of the next novel he completed, *On the Road*. The first full typescript of *On the Road* consisted not of individual sheets of typing paper but a taped-together continuous roll, approximately 120 feet long. He had typed *On the Road* onto this scroll very rapidly over a three week period in April 1951. By using a continuous roll of paper he could type uninterruptedly. When he unfurled this 'scroll' in front of his editor the latter's response—perhaps understandably—was to question whether such a typescript could possibly be edited. At the mention of the idea that he should make any changes, Kerouac rolled up his typescript and left; quite simply, he had never envisaged it being edited at all.

This led to a very long delay in getting *On the Road* published. First completed in 1951, the book did not appear until 1957. In the intervening period, ironically, Kerouac did in fact constantly revise and rewrite the novel. At one point during 1952 these constant rewrites had transformed much of the book into something else—so much so that Kerouac had enough material to assemble a completely different, parallel text. When he finally did this *Visions of Cody* was born, only for this new work also to be deemed unpublishable by almost everyone who read it until after his death

This sorry yet exciting saga of rejection, delay, compromise and enormously energetic writing activity soon soured Kerouac's relationship with the American publishing industry. And this souring meant that, even as he was rapidly composing a series of seven extraordinary works in the early fifties (*Doctor Sax*, *Maggie Cassidy*, 'The Railroad Earth', *The Subterraneans*, *Visions of Gerard*, *Tristessa* and part of *Old Angel Midnight*), almost none of his writing was being published. As a consequence, Kerouac effectively became independent of the constraints imposed on preparing books for publication. The commercial considerations that publishers tended to insist on did not impinge much on how he wrote. Consequently, in their different ways, each of these seven works, plus *Visions of Cody* and (to a lesser extent since it was constantly being revised) *On the Road*, became daring experiments, in which each explores ways of transmitting memory and experience as directly as possible.

His determination to try never to edit extended to how he typed out his memories (Kerouac was famous for the exactness of his memory, hence his nickname, 'Memory Babe'). Lucien Carr commented that Kerouac 'had a memory like few men that you meet', whilst Joyce Glassman described it as a 'minute memory'.[3] Relatedly, Kerouac sought never to edit what he wrote, never to omit nor ameliorate episodes or sentiments which might show him in a poor light. As he put it, 'the best writing is always the most painful personal wrung-out tossed from ... protective mind ... always honest'.[4] In this way, his writing can be thought of as 'confessional'.

This reminds us that Kerouac was brought up as a Catholic and that, though he did not remain an active church member, he never fully abandoned his Catholicism, even when embracing Buddhism in the 1950s. This provides a context for understanding the confessional reflexes running through his writing, and his disturbingly frank narrators are best understood in this confessional light.

This confessional tendency in his writing also alerts us to his French-Canadian identity. Kerouac was brought up in a steadily declining, middle-class, Catholic family in French-Canadian Lowell, Massachusetts. But he also mixed day-to-day with the children of Lowell's textile millworkers, in a working-class community known as *les blancs negres*.

Speaking French as his first language, Kerouac decidedly did not belong to the dominant group of White Anglo-Saxon Protestants (WASPs) still in command of America. Indeed, as his family grew poorer, and as he later became involved with New York City's underground, he became ever more alienated from many of the values of a WASP America inclined to stigmatize such origins and involvements.

This alienation helped him reflect skeptically on how to go about fictionalizing his experiences. What he determined to do after completing *The Town and the City* was to seek to develop a new, *spontaneous* prose style, as he called it. Yet we should remember that Kerouac was also, despite his protestations, a careful reviser of his work. He was, simply put, 'good [at] revision', as Malcolm Cowley, his most famous editor, once observed.[5]

Suggesting Kerouac was good at revision may seem like apostasy, since Kerouac himself was constantly asserting how important it was for a writer to write '"without consciousness in semi-trance" ... allowing sub-conscious to admit in own uninhibited ... "modern" language what conscious art would censor'.[6] He certainly always made an effort to shun repression, evasion, and inhibition when telling his story about living adventurously in post-war America. Kerouac above all wanted to excise self-censorship in his constant search for painful honesty. For him, this entailed rapid composition and an openness to what is often left repressed. This openness demanded constant practice at rapid composition—speed-writing in order to break through the filter of self-censorship that might otherwise intervene. Kerouac imposed on himself a discipline of constant writing practice, typing at enormous speed, until he developed an extraordinary facility. John Clellon Holmes described it as follows:

> [Jack] was a lightning typist ... [able to] disassociate from his fingers [to record] the movie in his head.... Jack said, 'Let's write a letter to Alan Harrington.' And I said, 'What do you mean?' He said 'Well, you do the first page, dictate to me, and I'll take it down on the typewriter, and then I'll do the same with you.' And literally ... he took it down, just as I talked to him. I tried to do it—I'm a very fast but inexact typist—and I couldn't come anywhere close.[8]

An astonishing directness resulted. Kerouac called it 'telepathic shock and meaning-excitement'.[9] At its best in his works written in the early fifties, *meaning-shock*, as I want to call it, is just what the reader receives. Yet the reader also encounters a writer frustrated in such a quest and contemplating the resulting frustration.

As Kerouac declined as a writer, ever more undermined by alcoholism and drug abuse, he increasingly spoke of wanting to put all his writings together as an integrated whole—what he called his 'Duluoz Legend'. This takes its name from the most common pseudonym given to the narrator in Kerouac's fiction, Jack Duluoz (other names used include Sal Paradise, Leo Percepied, Jacky, Ray Smith and—in rare instances—'Jack Kerouac'). Early on in his writing career, when serving as a merchant seaman during World War Two, Kerouac conceived of the idea of organizing his books into a saga (one initial inspiration for this approach was, in fact, John Galsworthy's *Forsyte Saga*), and he returned to this idea of creating a Duluoz saga increasingly often during his life. Yet it is really only his later novels that seek to realize this vision and establish a set of books linked up together. To an important extent these later writings, like *The Dharma Bums*, *Desolation Angels*, *Big Sur*, and *Satori in Paris* do hang together. Above all, they share similar narrative structures, each based upon the perspective of a self-doubting narrator. Furthermore, late in his life he wrote *Vanity of Duluoz* in large part as an attempt to patch up the 'holes'—the omissions—left in the account of Duluoz/Kerouac's life in his earlier writings—and in this way to show how there was indeed an evolving *Duluoz Legend*. (These 'holes' mostly centre upon his experiences in New York after he first left home to go to college and during the war years.) However, it must be added that the works that fit least securely into this Duluoz legend—mostly his early writings (particularly those in which the narrator is *not* called Jack Duluoz)—often contain better writing than those written with the Duluoz saga fully in mind.

If I were to stress how Kerouac's books could be read as a 'saga', then I would need to pick out how certain key events crop up in his writing more than once: his break-up with his closest adolescent sweetheart, Mary Carney; his failure to quite make the grade as an American football player at college; his peripheral involvement in a murder (David Kammerer's death at the hands of Kerouac's friend, Lucien Carr) and his subsequent arrest; the period of his life when he was closest to his buddy, Neal Cassady; and his spell as a lone fire-lookout on Desolation Peak in the Cascade mountains.

Each of these events constitutes a lynch-pin around which the Duluoz saga pivots. Kerouac's books can indeed be read as an ordered saga in this way (see Appendix B.i). But in the end, this sort of emphasis demands the introduction of constant cross-referencing, both between different books written at quite different times and between these books and Kerouac's life. Many other critics have undertaken this task. What I want to seek out is a more direct approach—both to his life on the one hand and his writing on the other. Consequently, as my brief account of Kerouac's life unfolds, it merely indicates in parentheses (in bold print), which book or books deal with the period of his life under examination, rather than mapping out any 'saga' and how it relates to his life.

Thus Kerouac's travels backwards and forwards across America with Neal Cassady are accompanied by the words ***On the Road***, his adventures with Gary Snyder by the words ***Dharma Bums***, and so on. This provides a bare indication of the close correlation between Kerouac's life and the subject-matter of his novels, but no more. In parallel with this, in a series of shaded text inserts, each of his major pieces of writing is briefly introduced. These introductions provide a short account of each work, accompanied by a brief assessment of the work's main characteristics. Their positioning coincides with the period in his life when he was just completing the work in question. However, these can be passed over if the reader wants to concentrate upon Kerouac's life alone. For a similar reason, rather than constantly interrupting my account of his life to explain the identities of the various pseudonymous characters in his fiction, I have instead appended a key to this study which indicates who Kerouac's major fictional characters were in life (Appendix A).

Kerouac did not solely write fiction. He also composed poetry, essays, Buddhist exegeses and other types of writing. My biography pays some attention to these and in a few specific instances ('The Railroad Earth', *Old Angel Midnight* and *Satori in Paris*) explores how Kerouac's fiction overlaps, as it were, the writing of poetry or autobiographical memoir. Nevertheless, the main focus of this study remains Kerouac's fiction, for which he is (rightly) most famous.

On the Road continues to be regarded as one of the most significant works of the twentieth century. I would argue, as well, that Jack Kerouac is one of the most significant novelists of the twentieth century—an unremittingly honest experimenter struggling to understand the cultural complexities of post-war America without simplification or schematization whilst simultaneously discovering how any such objective is always compromised. This is a demanding, contradictory goal for a writer to set himself, so some of his writing makes for demanding reading. But it is always rewarding, absorbing, and thought-provoking. Kerouac consistently offers an acute response to his life and times, drawing upon his use of 'deep form'. Truman Capote, in the mid-nineteen fifties, accused Kerouac of not writing but typing. I would argue that this intended insult is in fact a kind of compliment, recognizing how Kerouac moved writing on, taking it decisively beyond the pen-and-ink age and fully into the age of the typewriter by employing his skill at typing—at breakneck speed—in order to search for a way to take writing outside of its usual constraints and publishing proprieties. Kerouac opened his writing to the air—be this city air, Western air, or just *the* air. Kerouac offers us, in this sense, *outside writing*—outside conventional writing and its 'tea party ironies' (to use John Clellon Holmes' phrase).[10] Hence the title of this biography.

Chapter One: Beginnings

'I know how to ... write stories, and that's all'. (Kerouac, 1968[1])

Jack Kerouac was born in 1922 into a family of Roman Catholic, French-Canadian immigrants, who joined a large, long-lasting migration of French-Canadians from Quebec province into New England, mostly caused by a steady decline in French Canada's agricultural fortunes (as narrated in ***The Town and the City***). The Kerouac family settled eventually in Lowell, Massachusetts, where Kerouac was born. According to Kerouac himself, the Kerouac family (actually spelt Kéroack) traced its ancestry all the way back to Brittany, perhaps to a Breton baron from Cornwall, and even to Ireland. Indeed, genealogists, improving on his research, have suggested he is related to both Hilary Clinton and Camilla Parker Bowles. Another of Kerouac's claims was that the first man to set foot in America from this family, the Lebris de Kerouacs, had arrived in Quebec 'to help Montcalm fight Wolfe', and then married an Iroquois (the first of several such intermarriages, Kerouac believed).[2] On his mother's side, Kerouac claimed the Lévesque family was Norman French.

Much of this is not fact but legend, however. The Kerouac family originated from the Kervoacs, a cluster of hamlets on the south-eastern edge of the town of Lanmeur, not far from Morlaix, a port on the Brittany coast. What is also known for sure is that the Kirouack/Kéroack family, potato farmers in Quebec province during the late nineteenth century, became economic migrants, traveling to Nashua, New Hampshire shortly after the birth of Kerouac's father, Leo, in 1889. Leo at first worked in Nashua's mills, but then learned the printing trade and was taken on as an apprentice printer. He moved to Lowell in 1912 to work on the newspaper, *L'Étoile*. Leo married Gabrielle Lévesque (another Catholic, born in Quebec) in 1915: François Gerard was their first son (1916), Caroline (Ti Nin) their only daughter (1918). Jean-Louis Kerouac (also known as Ti Jean, and later as Jack Kerouac) was born on 12 March 1922. Gerard, however, died young of rheumatic fever in 1926 to the sorrow of the family. Gabrielle, a devout

Catholic, and Jack both regarded Gerard as saintly and were particularly distressed by his death (as retold in ***Visions of Gerard***; ***The Town and the City***).

After Gerard's death Leo turned increasingly to drink and gambling, and the resulting family arguments led Jack to retreat into playing private, elaborate, self-invented games and to grow even closer to his mother, whom he called Mémêre (see ***The Town and the City***; ***Doctor Sax***). As family fortunes declined owing to Leo's neglect of his printing business, the family moved from Centralville, Lowell to Pawtucketville (the part known as 'Little Canada'—a rather poorer neighborhood in Lowell). Eventually Gabrielle even needed to take up millwork (as retold in ***The Town and the City***). At school Kerouac was at first quite successful but because of the family move to Pawtucketville he was transferred from the French-speaking school where he had begun his studies to another, English-speaking one. Up until then (1933) he had been taught in French and spoke a type of French-Canadian known as joual. At his new school Kerouac found things difficult at first but in due course he settled in, composing a short story that his teacher identified as 'brilliant'.[3] He also started spending time at his father's print shop where he began to develop his phenomenal typing skills.

Just after Gerard's death Kerouac began to dream-up in his head pantomime-movies, and then to write his own comic-strips and mystery magazines (as narrated in ***Doctor Sax***). Aged only eleven, he also composed a novel influenced by *Huckleberry Finn* called *Mike Explores the Merrimack* (as narrated in ***The Town and the City***). He also began to devise elaborate games based on baseball and horse racing (see ***The Town and the City***; ***Doctor Sax***) and to play pranks, dressed as a masked 'Shadow' character, inspired by pulp magazine characters such as the *Phantom Detective* and *The Shadow* (as retold in ***Doctor Sax***).

The decline of Kerouac's father's printing business accelerated when Lowell was hit by a massive flood caused by the Potomac breaking its banks in 1936 (as retold in ***Doctor Sax***; ***The Town and the City***). In its aftermath Jack turned increasingly to a growing circle of friends, who nicknamed him 'Memory Babe' because of his feats of memory.[4] He also developed a deep love of American popular music at this time (particularly a passion for Glen Miller). This linked up with his well-established love of the movies and cartoon comic-books to ensure Kerouac's lively imagination was deeply engaged with 1930s' US popular culture. He also took up seriously a range of sporting activities. Able enough at baseball, he proved particularly skilful at track running (see ***Maggie Cassidy***) and football (see ***The Town and the City***; ***Vanity of Duluoz***). Even as his father's business crumbled away, pushing Leo into bankruptcy in 1937, Jack's sporting fortunes rose. He became a skilful young sportsman, even attracting the attention of varsity coaches, though he had trouble

Jack Kerouac playing American football, a sports photograph in the *Lowell Sun* 25 November 1938.

making the High School football team, either because he was tactically withheld as a surprise weapon to be introduced during key plays, or because inter-communal jealousies in Lowell influenced his football coach's selections, or both (as retold in ***The Town and the City***; ***Vanity of Duluoz***). In parallel, he remained scholastically successful and began reading voraciously (including Goethe, Victor Hugo, H. G. Wells, Emily Dickinson, Tolstoy, Walt Whitman, Hemingway and, a little later, Thomas Wolfe).

Kerouac also began writing seriously—primarily at this time composing short stories, encouraged by a school friend, Sammy Sampas, who introduced him into his Junior High school's elite literary club, called the Scribbler's. Sampas also introduced him to the work of William Saroyan, whom he greatly admired (see ***Vanity of Duluoz***). His cultural interests remained eclectic, however: he also at about this time became a keen fan of Swing bands (especially Benny Goodman).

1938 was also the year he began to date: after learning how to jive from two boys who used drugs (marijuana and benzedrine), he attended a local dance where he met and started going out with an Irish-American girl called Mary Carney (as retold in ***Maggie Cassidy***). He also two-timed her with another Lowell girl, Margaret (Peggy) Coffey, whilst Mary, realizing his lack of interest in marriage, began dating other boys. Kerouac drifted between Peggy and Mary, continuing to see Peggy whilst increasingly desiring to marry Mary, just as she (ironically) was turning away from him. He also indulged in some light homosocial sexual play and even, perhaps, some homosexual liaisons. At this point Kerouac's double-dating dilemmas were somewhat fortuitously resolved: in 1938 he won a college football scholarship—at Columbia University. The University's entrance requirements compelled him to go to prep school—Horace Mann Prep—before he entered Columbia, so this also meant leaving Lowell and Mary and Peggy behind (as retold in ***Vanity of Duluoz; Maggie Cassidy; The Town and the City***).

Kerouac's move to New York on a sports scholarship in 1939 also ushered in a period in which he combined diverse reading (particularly classic French authors in the original) with sports—both track and football. However, he mixed slightly uneasily with the group of students from wealthier backgrounds that he met at Horace Mann. As Clellon Holmes points out, his 'people' would first and foremost always be those that 'worked blue-collar jobs; they were Saturday night people'.[5] Yet he could also embrace his new New York life, developing, for example, his interest in jazz. He visited many of New York's jazz clubs, where he especially enjoyed Count Basie's orchestra, which at the time featured Lester Young (see ***Vanity of Duluoz***; ***The Town and the City***). He even wrote about jazz in the Horace Mann newspaper, the *Record*, and interviewed Glenn Miller in June 1940. During visits to the nearby jazz joints he also tried marijuana and benzedrine—given him by some of the African-American musicians he befriended. Through such contacts he became an early fan of 'bop', as this began to emerge as a jazz form in the early 1940s.

He also continued to develop as a writer, composing short stories showing the influence of Hemingway, Thoreau and

Thomas Hardy for the school's literary magazine, the *Horace Mann Quarterly*. His contributions included a detective story, 'The Brothers', in 1939 and, in the following year, 'Une Veille de Noel', featuring the appearance of Christ to a group of drinkers. These first publication successes helped develop his desire to become a writer. However, the resulting new interests and orientations ensured that he saw himself moving away from the type of safe domestic life in Lowell desired by Mary Carney, and they separated further, step by step (as retold in ***Maggie Cassidy***). Far from wanting to settle down, Kerouac turned to increasing drug abuse of various sorts, and to viewing himself as an apprentice writer.

Between finishing at Horace Mann Prep and going up to Columbia, Kerouac returned to Lowell and cultivated some new friends, including a literary-oriented coterie into which Sammy Sampas introduced him. This group furthered his interest in Whitman, Saroyan, Wolfe and the romantic poets (Byron and Shelley in particular). Jack London also became a major inspiration. Up at Columbia he played football, got injured and continued reading voraciously (as retold in ***The Town and the City***; ***Vanity of Duluoz***). Yet Thomas Wolfe remained his firm favorite, so when he began writing more often he produced 'long Wolfean stories'.[6] He also became sufficiently popular to be elected vice-president of the Columbia sophomore class. But he flunked chemistry, and instead of revising for his chemistry re-sit that summer, he preferred listening to jazz music (Artie Shaw), cinema-going, further reading (Dos Passos, Joyce) and generally larking around. He was also still intermittently seeing and sleeping with Peggy Coffey and spasmodically pursuing his desire to be a writer (as retold in ***Vanity of Duluoz***). He even found enough time to produce one short story, which featured a wild prophet preaching in Times Square (much later this story-line was partly integrated into his novella, *Pic*).

Back at College (1940-41) his interest in football waned, but his reading (especially Tolstoy), and a friendship with Henri Cru, whom he had met at Horace Mann, both blossomed. He dropped out of College (having not made good his chemistry fail) and, whilst holding down dead-end jobs, began writing in earnest, working on a novel and putting together a collection of short stories, *Atop an Underwood*,[7] over-indebted to Wolfe, Hemingway and Saroyan. (This title was later used for a rather different collection of early apprentice works published in 1999 long after Kerouac's death.) He also read Dostoyevsky (*Notes from the Underground*), more books by James Joyce (*Ulysses*, especially Molly's stream-of-consciousness soliloquy), and further work by Saroyan and Dos Passos. Obtaining a job as a sports columnist on the *Lowell Sun*, Kerouac also started his first novel, *Vanity of Duluoz* (1941), a shapeless James Joyce-influenced work only very distantly related to the book of this title published nearly two decades later.

At this time—the early 1940s—Kerouac's life lacked clear direction, and the onset of World War Two stimulated a new rootlessness: he drifted down to Washington, DC in late 1942 and there started drinking quite heavily. However, he soon returned to New York and entered his first major relationship since leaving Lowell. Through Horace Cru he had earlier met up with a woman called Edie Parker in New York. Now, at a time when he was engaging in passing sex with both men and women, he also struck up seriously with Edie. They soon broke up and Kerouac returned to Lowell, further heavy drinking, and a lot of Benzedrine intake, before finally taking decisive action. He signed up for the US Merchant Marine, feeling he should join the war effort, and in mid-1942 joined the *SS Dorchester* (as retold in ***Vanity of Duluoz***; ***The Town and the City***). The *Dorchester* took him on a dangerous wartime voyage to Greenland. On the journey he read Thomas Mann, befriended an old Communist (the National Maritime Union still being, generally, a left-wing organization at this time)[8] and began to plan a long sea novel to be called *The Sea Is My Brother*. On his return he went back to Columbia, its football squad, his Columbia circle of friends and Mark Van Doren's classes.[9] He read Thorstein Veblen and worked further on *The Sea Is My Brother*, which began to take shape as a Melville-influenced naturalistic sea saga of merchant marine life.

At this point World War Two intervened in his life decisively: he received his navy call-up, failed a medical and was sent to boot camp in March 1943. He disliked this experience so intensely that he sought to manipulate his discharge by faking insanity. His efforts bore fruit, for finally he was sent to a navy mental hospital. There, he met and befriended a character called William Holmes Hubbard, nicknamed 'Big Slim'. After some psychological assessments in this navy hospital, Kerouac was honorably discharged from the navy as of 'indifferent character' (as retold in ***The Town and the City***; ***Vanity of Duluoz***).

By now the Kerouac family home had shifted to New York, his parents having moved there to be closer to their children after Leo's bankruptcy left them with no reason to remain in Lowell. Kerouac, however, was still footloose. He signed up on the *USS George Weems*, and after another fling with Edie and a drunken binge with Hubbard, he sailed in August 1943 for Liverpool. He was still working on *The Sea Is My Brother*, but during the voyage, inspired by John Galsworthy's *Forsyte Saga*, he also began to conceive of a series of interconnected novels depicting his life, intended to stand as a 'contemporary history record'[10] (as retold in ***Vanity of Duluoz***). This idea was a seeding-ground for his later desire to write a series of interlinked novels about his life. His visit to Liverpool was brief, and centered upon a trip to London, a liaison with a Liverpudlian prostitute, and the writing of a fiction piece, 'The Romanticist', in port.

By October 1943 the *USS George Weems* had returned to New York. Kerouac briefly rejoined his family before moving out to live with Edie, whose room-mate was Joan Vollmer Adams (see ***Vanity of Duluoz***; ***The Town and City***). During 1943 and 1944 he continued to try to develop his writing career. He read *Finnegan's Wake*, and wrote fiction and newspaper articles at great speed. He also developed his love affair with American popular culture: going to the movies, expanding his taste for bop (Slam Stewart first; then later, Charlie Parker, Dizzy Gillespie, and Coleman Hawkins), and meeting many new NYC bohemians through his city friends. Amongst these new acquaintances was a young man, Lucien Carr and the circle Carr moved in. Carr introduced Kerouac to Allen Ginsberg with whom a close friendship rapidly formed. Another of Carr's acquaintances, David Kammerer, a homosexual with a sexual fixation on Carr, introduced Kerouac to William Burroughs, at the time already an experienced experimenter with drugs. This new bohemian circle introduced him to the work of Rimbaud, Baudelaire, Lautrémont, Apollinaire, Rilke and Nietzsche. He became deeply influenced by a symbolist aesthetic exemplified by Baudelaire's lines from his poem, 'Le Voyage': 'plonger au fond du gouffre,/ Enfer ou Ciel, qu'importe?' (dive to the very bottom of the abyss/ Hell or Heaven, whatever?—*Les Fleurs du Mal*, 1861).[11]

A number of Kerouac's new acquaintances were homosexual (including Ginsberg, Burroughs and Kammerer). Kerouac had already had homosexual experiences, during adolescent play in Lowell, during his time in the merchant marine, and also intermittently in New York, though what is best described as his bisexuality predominantly expressed itself through heterosexual activities. He was, however, very far from stable (socially, sexually or in terms of his ambitions). He was instead, by 1944, leading a chaotic lifestyle, marked by much alcohol and drug abuse. The only stability was provided by his continuing writing. This was becoming increasingly experimental in its approach, and influenced by his love of bebop improvisation—the first seeds of his embrace of a 'spontaneous bop prosody'.

The inside front cover of *Vanity of Duluoz* (1968), featuring pictures from Kerouac's family photo albums.

All the chaos around him came home to roost when Lucien Carr felt it necessary to kill David Kammerer in 1944 because, he claimed, Kammerer's sexual obsession with him was becoming increasingly oppressive and threatening. Another version of the story depicts Kammerer as the victim of Carr's selfishness. Whatever the truth, Carr involved Kerouac in the aftermath of the murder by asking him to help hide the weapon he had used, and this led to Kerouac's brief imprisonment as an 'accessory' after the truth inevitably came out. Kerouac found he could only raise bail by marrying Edie

Parker since his own father refused to help him, disliking his new circle of friends (as narrated in ***The Town and the City***; ***Vanity of Duluoz***).

For a while—following what amounted to his enforced marriage to Edie in August 1944—Kerouac settled down somewhat, reading and writing with renewed vigor at Grosse Pointe where Edie's family lived. But eventually he returned to New York (in October 1944) and soon signed up for another sea voyage, this time on the *SS Robert Treat Paine*. However, he did not enjoy the voyage (he was ostracized and bullied) and jumped ship in Norfolk, Virginia. Back in New York he holed up in solitude to start writing seriously (chiefly working on *The Sea Is My Brother*), and to read yet more (mostly Nietzsche, Rimbaud, Goethe, Rilke). He called this period his search for 'Self-Ultimacy'—a search at one point involving him using his own blood as ink. William Burroughs tracked him down and helped rescue him from this Rimbaud-and-Nietzsche inspired blind-alley which had even led him to decide to burn everything he wrote (as retold in ***Vanity of Duluoz***).

Burroughs now became his mentor, lecturing him on Korzybskian linguistics, and lending him books from his library (Stephen Crane, Céline, Cocteau, Dashiell Hammett, James M. Cain and Spengler's *Decline of the West*).[12] Kerouac also undertook some study of the gnostics and Zen Buddhism (at the suggestion of a tutor on a Columbia University course he was taking, Raymond Weaver). He also became part of a newly-forming bohemian circle. Drugs (especially benzedrine) were used heavily, and Burroughs, Ginsberg and Kerouac participated in periods of psychoanalytic 'free-association'. Kerouac at this time also became more openly (but also guiltily) bisexual.

Kerouac was not unlike many young men and women in this period who found it difficult to settle down. This restlessness resulted from the disruptions to their lives created by participating in the war effort—often on active service or as footloose participants in the war effort and war industries, or through adolescent experience of the consequences of these changes and disruptions. During these years America's larger cities—particularly New York—saw the influx of a constantly changing population of young people on leave from the army or moving in search of or between jobs in a thriving wartime economy. It was a period in which unemployment fell to levels that would have been unimaginably low only ten years previously, in the 1930s, when America had been gripped by a deep recession. Some of these wartime young men and women were visiting a large city for a prolonged period for the first time, and many of them (the more adventurous) encountered cultures and lifestyles that fundamentally changed their outlook on life. Their self-definitions, their understanding of themselves, of their 'place', and of how they could act, all changed. Very often this mostly young segment of society re-examined their assumptions about morality, their understanding of their sexuality, and their comprehension of their role in society (especially as previously prescribed—or even proscribed—by their gender). Simply put, many men and women began to redefine themselves—how they should live, and what their relationship to their society should be. One sign of these adjustments was the openness that Alfred Kinsey encountered during his sexological research at this time. Though homosexuals were commonly bracketed with Communists as undesirables at the time, Kinsey, throughout the period 1945 to 1946, was researching male sexual behavior and discovering homosexuality to be a more widespread practice than had been previously realized—or, at least, accepted. During his interviewing sessions in Greenwich Village, Kinsey interviewed Allen Ginsberg, William Burroughs, and, according to some commentators, Jack Kerouac as well.[13] Kinsey consequently even gets a mention in *On the Road*.

Kerouac was, then, very much a confused and excited member of this group of mid-century young people. Because he had previously lived in New York after winning a sports scholarship, he was well situated to explore to the full this exciting, if confusing, late-wartime and post-wartime cultural environment. It might loosely be described as bohemian—though I think this word fails to quite capture its diversity. It was a culture embracing not just a population of highly excited—and, very often, over-excited—young people, but also a twilight world of urban misfits, hangers-on, delinquents and petty and not-so-petty criminals. Prominent in this harlequin underground were aspiring writers and artists, and Kerouac now identified himself as one of these.

Chapter Two: From *The Town and the City* to *On the Road*

In May 1945 during an extended period of drug taking, alcohol excess and amateur psycho-analysis with Burroughs and Ginsberg, Kerouac conceived of and, probably soon afterwards, began work on what would become his first published novel, *The Town and the City* (originally entitled "Galloway"). By now intent on becoming a writer, Kerouac in the early Summer of 1945 also begun yet another novel (this time cooperatively with Burroughs—each writing a chapter in turn). Entitled *And the Hippos Were Boiled in Their Tanks*, it was a Hammettesque murder-mystery, fictionalizing the Carr-Kammerer case (but published only in 2008). At about this time, Edie Parker came back to Kerouac in New York and they moved into Joan Vollmer Adams' apartment, along with Burroughs. There the trio had many visitors, frequently including a new acquaintance from Denver, Hal Chase, a prostitute associate of his called Vicki Russell, and a small-time crook, Herbert Huncke, who had introduced Burroughs to heroin and was to feature in Burroughs' first book, *Junkie: Confessions of an Unredeemed Drug Addict* (published in 1953 under the name of William Lee). Around this time Kerouac also began thinking about and perhaps working on a new, significantly different version of *Vanity of Duluoz*.

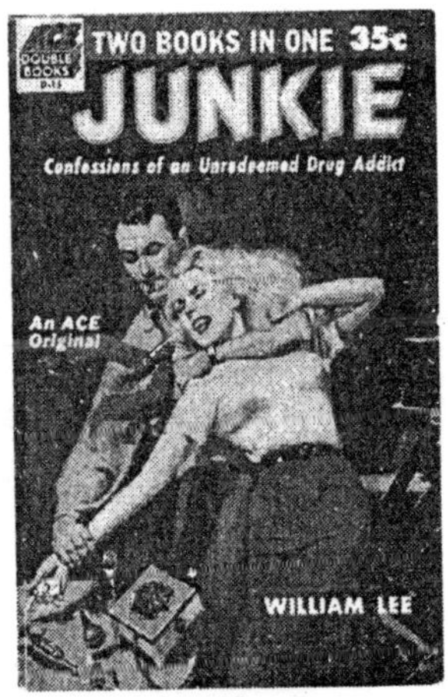

Front cover to Ace Books' edition of William Lee [William Burroughs], *Junkie*. Ace specialised in mass market paperbacks, as this cover design suggests.

Kerouac was now writing with great speed and frequency. Céline, Dostoyevsky and James Joyce (particularly the complex effects of Joyce's verbal juggling) remained great influences, alongside Thomas Wolfe (as always). Kerouac was selecting his reading with meticulous care for the help it would provide him as he struggled to develop his writing style.

When writing at this time Kerouac often composed in great rushes, either composing spontaneously or typing out pre-prepared scenes, set up in his head in advance and mulled-over intermittently until they gelled. Such experimentation with spontaneous or breakneck composition became progressively more important to him in this period. He also worked on more overtly commercial pieces whilst he shared with Ginsberg what they both called 'visions' of New York, through which they moved like phantoms (possibly an inspiration for the scene in *On the Road* in which Ed Dunkel feels he has become a ghost on Times Square—*OR*, 108).

This period in his life was an important turning point for Kerouac. For the first time his self-abusive lifestyle seriously impacted on his health. He contracted acute phlebitis, caused primarily by heavy benzedrine abuse, after Vicki Russell had introduced him to the technique of breaking open benzedrine inhalers. He was also trying to negotiate between his attraction to and repulsion from (and distrust of) Ginsberg. Perhaps as a reaction, he also began to have more to do with Hal Chase, captivated by his mid-west origins and what Kerouac saw as his consequent romantic hopefulness. Chase made Kerouac aware of a difference between himself and Burroughs and Ginsberg (perhaps rooted in the latter pair's more decisively homosexual propensities). Chase saw himself and Kerouac as pure (Western) Wolfeans compared to the others' Baudelairean devotion to stylized (Eastern) decadence (see ***The Town and the City***). Kerouac's father's dislike of Ginsberg and his circle perhaps exacerbated the feeling Kerouac had developed of a social and aesthetic divide, cleaving his friends apart along these lines, especially since Leo was at the time (1944-46) dying of cancer.

It was above all Leo's death in 1946 that makes this period such an important turning point in Kerouac's life. *And the Hippos Were Boiled in Their Tanks*, the experiment he worked on with Burroughs, had been quickly finished. But when submitted to publishers it was rejected—causing a short period of writer's block. Leo's death, however, stimulated Kerouac to start writing again. It also caused him to become less dilettante and to focus upon one project: a novel that would develop into *The Town and the City*. He now wrote with great rapidity: both his father's death and the funeral in early 1946 reinforced his sense that he was embarked on a new, meaningful voyage—a commitment to writing as a career (as retold in ***The Town and the City***; ***Vanity of Duluoz***).

This turning point by way of his friendship with Hal Chase led Kerouac in one further decisive direction. Through Chase and a friend of Chase, Justin Brierly, Kerouac had begun to hear about Neal Cassady, a Denver juvenile delinquent, bisexual confidence trickster and allegedly avid reader (of, it was said, Kant, Schopenhauer, Nietzsche, Shakespeare and Dostoyevsky). Neal aroused Jack's interest because he came from the West and because of his background. When Chase returned West, he showed Neal some of Jack's letters, so stimulating a reciprocal interest in Kerouac. Jack meantime met Ed White, another of Brierly's friends from Denver. The Midwest was beginning to enter his life.

All these Denver contacts meant that when Neal Cassady came to New York in December 1946 with his newly-wed wife, LuAnne, an encounter with Kerouac was inevitable. In New York, Neal first established a rapport with Ginsberg, before meeting and befriending Jack. Cassady had an immediate effect on Kerouac—as on almost everyone he met. Joan Haverty, for example, on her first (somewhat later) meeting with Neal in 1951 was bowled over by his talk of 'cars and escapades, jail memories and women and nights and blues'.[14] *On the Road* provides a more or less detailed account of Cassady's effect on Kerouac and their relationship over the next few years, except for editing out their very first encounter (see ***On the Road***; ***Visions of Cody***).

Neal Cassady, after conducting an intense affair with Ginsberg, soon returned to Denver in pursuit of LuAnne who, feeling neglected as Cassady raced about, had already left New York. The long letter Cassady wrote about his journey back in 1947 deeply influenced Kerouac because of its directness and lack of literary sophistication (it was full of poor grammar, misspellings and crossings-out). The letter became known in Kerouac's circle as 'the great sex letter': it did indeed detail Cassady's sexual peccadilloes. But what was to be more important for Kerouac was the style in which it was written:

> Without the slightest preliminaries or objective remarks (what's your name? where are you going? etc.) I plunged into a

> completely knowing, completely subjective, personal & so to speak "penetrating her core" way of speech; to be shorter (since I'm getting unable to write) by 2 A.M. I had her swearing eternal love, complete subjectivity to me & immediate satisfaction. I, anticipating even more pleasure, wouldn't allow her to blow me on the bus, instead we played, as they say, with each other.... when we arrived at St. Louis at 4 A.M.... She (note the capital) claimed her bag & retired to the toilet to change —— long dash —— / This next paragraph must, of necessity, be written completely objectively ——[15]

Even in this short extract, Cassady introduces both an intense self-consciousness and a hint of his own unreliability (This next paragraph must, of necessity, be written completely objectively'), qualities later found in Kerouac's writing. Despite its clichéd style, the letter's unconventional syntax, its sense of language as inadequate and its use of the demotic slang (such as obscenities) meant it possessed affinities with what is known in jazz as 'scat' (improvised singing). Both scat and Cassady's style were now to become influences on Kerouac. In subsequent correspondence between them in this period, Kerouac is plainly ever more blown away by Cassady's raw writing style, seeing in it a new kind of 'spontaneity' which he felt he could exploit to further his own writing. But even Neal's own writing could not, for Joan Haverty, 'capture the vitality and intensity of the voice I ... heard, describing everything in such a way that I lived it just by listening ... I became aware of his ability to perceive an event on several different levels at once'.[16]

Kerouac, too, was somewhat over-awed but, though Cassady affected his writing style immediately, this effect was not consistent. Rather, Kerouac also continued working hard on writing *The Town and the City*, still to remain more conventionally composed than the sort of experimentation that Cassady's prose stimulated. The novel was now progressing only slowly in marked contrast to the speed Kerouac brought to much of his other writing by which he began to be increasingly diverted. In a real sense his admiration for Cassady's 1947 letter on the one hand and his more or less Wolfean prose-writing central to *The Town and the City* on the other were pulling him in different directions. One style was quite consciously literary, the other, above all, valued spontaneity—'scribbling'.

Perhaps this division in his writing approach helped provoke Kerouac to leave New York. A meeting with Horace Cru and an offer by Cru of a place on a ship's crew in San Francisco, however, precipitated Kerouac's departure westwards in 1947 (see ***On the Road***). En route he also knew he could visit Denver and meet up with his circle of Denver friends, especially as Allen Ginsberg had joined Cassady there. At this time, both on his transcontinental journey and when in Denver, Kerouac began to keep notebooks—a habit he consistently kept up for the rest of his life. In these notebooks he jotted his moment-to-moment 'visions', important sources for his evolving writing style. Lucien Carr later recalled that Kerouac 'always found time to scrawl in the little books'.[17] He made notes, for example, about his attempt to hitch out of New York, his eventual resort to a bus to Chicago and then the details of his long hitchhike from Chicago to Denver.

In Denver, Kerouac indeed discovered a gulf opening up between the more bourgeois writers in his circle of acquaintance, such as Ed White, on the one hand, and Neal and a Neal-besotted Ginsberg on the other (as retold in ***On the Road***). Jack oscillated between the two groups, but also felt attracted by Neal's new girlfriend, Carolyn. His final allegiance largely shifted to Neal's 'party' during a series of adventures in Denver (including a relationship with a waitress called Helen Gullion), but he was also becoming very late for his rendezvous with Cru in San Francisco, so he quickly left Denver. In San Francisco, he found no ship lined up and Cru instead working as a security guard in seamen's barracks. For a while Kerouac took up the same job (effectively, working as a species of cop, though he quickly found he disliked it). The appeal of San Francisco soon petered out, and after completing a long, unsuccessful film script, Kerouac headed South, meeting a young Mexican girl (Bea Franco) in Bakersfield and living with her for two weeks in Los Angeles, Bakersfield and Selma (as retold in ***On the Road***). He then made his way back to his mother's house in New York, thereby completing the first of a number of round trips across America (see ***On the Road***; ***Visions of Cody***). Returning to Mémêre at the end of each adventure became a recurrent pattern in his life—a pattern later marked by an increasing sense of dependency upon her.

Back in New York in the autumn of 1947 Kerouac remained in contact with Cassady, whose letters urged him to abandon 'all rules, literary styles, and other such pretensions' and write 'in a continuous chain of undisciplined thought'.[18] Kerouac also wrote for long hours, working steadily on *The Town and the City*, more rapidly on other manuscripts—'spin-offs' from the main work or from each other. New York City life provided (often frantic) breaks from his writing. In New York he proved himself to be an attentive listener, both to jazz and the conversations around him. He also felt drawn to existentialism (led there by his reading of precursors like Céline and Kafka), and hence further away from the Catholic Church.

Kerouac also drew much at this time from his still skeptical friendship with Ginsberg. In particular, once *The Town and the City* was completed in 1948, Ginsberg, a busy literary networker, set about aiding him to get it placed with a publisher, only to be met with initial rejections: first by Scribner's, Thomas Wolfe's publishers, and then by Macmillan. Kerouac therefore began to try to concentrate on what he consequently saw as necessary revisions to *The Town and the City*. But he was also drawing closer to an expanding group of New York artistic bohemians. These met to talk, party and orgy at the apartment of Bill Cannastra who had befriended Kerouac earlier in 1948. Cannastra stimulated Kerouac's interest in blues and bluegrass as well as jazz. The blues in particular began to influence the way Kerouac wrote (particularly his poetry). Another important new friend was John Clellon Holmes, another writer, who also possessed useful publishing connections.

Arguably, Kerouac had by now shown he was able to sustain heterosexual relationships only poorly, perhaps instead deriving much of the female intimacy he needed from Mémere. The Cannastra-sponsored orgies provided an irregular (bi-)sexual outlet. This unhappy oscillation between a 'safe' home life with Mémere and a dissolute city life perhaps motivated his increasingly heavy drinking, though publishers' successive rejections of *The Town and the City*, and the resulting need to continuously revise it, played their part. Kerouac also enrolled on some NYC New School courses, one taught by Alfred Kazin and another on Creative Writing. The latter's tutor, Brom Weber, attacked *The Town and the City* as too Wolfean and incoherent, whilst Kerouac defended it and also, on another tack, urged the virtues of something akin to automatic writing. This, coupled with the novel's continuing rejection, meant that late 1948 became an agitated time for Kerouac, marked by 'paranoiac attacks'.[19] However, it also seems to have stung him into working on two new novels, one entitled *Doctor Sax: the Myth of the Rainy Night* and the other *On the Road*. The latter was conceived of as a sequel to *The Town and the City* and consequently at this time (late 1948) it bore little resemblance to what would in fact become his next major work: the confessional, autobiographical novel that emerged as *On the Road* in 1957.

Kerouac at this time started writing with considerably greater freedom. Even as he completed *The Town and the City* he was coming to regard his writing in this first novel as largely falling short of a new target—to concentrate upon writing faithfully about his immediate experience. It is observable that the later sections of *The Town and the City*, those treating with New York City, are largely written in a different style to that used to depict the town of 'Galloway'. The language register used to portray New York is less floridly romantic, and more factual, colloquial and demotic: the voice of the New York underground can begin to be heard. Kerouac, one senses, was excited by the new voice he was discovering and developing. The need to convey this voice's immediacy also resulted in an increasing tendency to adopt a first-person narrative voice (influenced once more by Cassady's letters). Kerouac's switch to writing first-person fiction at this time (the late 1940s) soon became decisive: almost all the prose he wrote thereafter was written as a first-person narrative (even *Pic* is first-person in form, though narrated by an African American boy).

At the same time—and plainly related—what he wrote drew ever more closely from incidents in his life. He strove for authenticity when depicting these incidents, but such attempts at total accuracy were very soon accompanied by a strong sense that, paradoxically, such accuracy would always be compromised. It would be compromised not just because of his own personality and beliefs, which Kerouac came to see would inevitably color what he wrote, but also because he recognized that his personality and beliefs were not simply and wholly 'his own', divorced from the society in which he had grown up and in which he lived. His ideas, his language, and his way of seeing things were a negotiation, an *arbitration* it might be said, between different forces: the influence of his family and upbringing; his experience of American culture—particularly popular culture; his reading; and his attraction to New York's artistic bohemia and the contacts it promoted with both criminal and drug undergrounds. Each of these helped shape his sense of his self and his identity (his subjectivity) often in conflicting ways, and this in turn, he saw, influenced how he expressed himself and how he wrote. His writing constantly confronts this recognition. And, as a consequence, authenticity emerges not as an unproblematic and unambiguous goal that can be attained, but as a multiple, shifting, dissonant kaleidoscope of perspectives—different 'takes'—on experience.

At about the same time, apparently paradoxically, he also began to talk of himself as a 'factualist', picking up a term used at the time by William Burroughs. But by 'factualism' Burroughs sought to denote a writing practice employing a hard-boiled style across both realistic depictions of material experience and a world of the imagination—dreams, nightmares, hallucinations and fantastic flights—so flattening out the distinction between the two. Artistically, all were to be treated as *facts*, all equally suitable subjects for what Burroughs called 'routines'—slightly wild, nightmarish imaginings, but ones written about in a cool, documentary prose. Kerouac's first attempts to depict his 1947 travels showed this influence, and his initial thinking about a new novel called *Doctor Sax* was much influenced by this approach (though also rooted in a renewed admiration for Melville and Shakespeare). At about this time, whilst recovering confidence artistically, Kerouac formed a series of (more or less precarious) heterosexual relationships. Usually the woman was required to assume the sexual initiative. He also had an argument (by correspondence) with Ginsberg concerning Kerouac's censorious attitude towards homosexuality.

Neal Cassady now (late 1948) joined Kerouac, traveling across the USA from San Francisco with Al and Helen Hinkle. Cassady caught up with Kerouac at his sister's house and helped him move her furniture to Ozone Park (as retold in ***On the Road***; ***Visions of Cody***). A drunken, hectic and often argumentative period in New York ensued (Cassady's class background fitting poorly into bohemian New York circles), though alleviated slightly by celebrations over the news that Kerouac's *The Town and the City* had been recommended by Alfred Kazin to Robert Giroux at the publishers, Harcourt Brace. Kerouac's breakthrough as a writer had begun.

Kerouac during this period (with Holmes and Al Hinkle in particular) often discussed the identity of the disparate circle he moved in, and began to define it as a '*beat* generation'.[20]

One facet of Kerouac's fame is the fact that he effectively christened the 'Beat Generation' at this time. What its naming as early as 1948 makes clear is that the term Beat Generation refers not to a 1950s' phenomenon but to the generation emerging during the closing years of World War Two and those that immediately followed. One marker of this generational change was Kerouac's suggestion that America was '"picking up"' and that the 'great American of the future' would be '"the hitchhiking Negro saint"'[21] (a suggestion containing further seeds for *Pic*). John Clellon Holmes felt there was an excitement around: 'Everyone I knew felt it ... that bottled eagerness for talk, for joy, for excitement, for sensation, for new truths ... everyone of my age had a look of impatience and expectation'.[22]

At this point, early in 1949, Kerouac, Cassady, LuAnne and Al Hinkle set off on the second transcontinental trip to feature in *On the Road*, firstly heading off to New Orleans to visit Burroughs (who had fled there from police harassment over his drug habit) and to pick up Hinkle's wife, Helen, abandoned there on Neal's West to East journey with the Hinkles to find Kerouac in late 1948 (as retold in ***On the Road***; ***Visions of Cody***). Hinkle and his wife elected to stay in New Orleans, so Kerouac, Cassady and LuAnne continued on to San Francisco alone. Immediately upon arrival, Cassady rather callously deserted them—though he did return after LuAnne separated from a penniless Jack. However, soon after Cassady had picked him up again, Kerouac, disenchanted with Cassady and still moneyless, decided to return East to New York, where he re-enrolled at the New School (see ***On the Road***; ***Visions of Cody***). All of these travels and travails are recorded in his detailed journals which contributed many seeds to *On the Road*. At this time Kerouac also resumed work on *Doctor Sax*, and began writing more poetry, concerned to secure 'the furthest possible reach of an idea ... on the edge of relative meaning' whilst also recognizing that the results might be 'loony'.[23] Spasmodically, he also worried over the proliferating narrative structure of what would become *On the Road*. To get things more under control, he foregrounded the first-person narrator more, at the time called Ray Smith, trying to turn him into 'the hero's [Sancho] Panza, the hero's Boswell, the hero's Pip'[24]—a complex figure whom he hoped might be able to draw together the multitude of characters and plot-lines of the novel.

In May 1949 the final publishing breakthrough occurred: definite acceptance of *The Town and the City* by Harcourt, Brace. Since this climactic moment was accompanied by the near-simultaneous but separate drugs-related arrests of both Burroughs and Ginsberg, Kerouac's life simplified somewhat. So when the publisher called for revisions Kerouac had the time to observe a punishing writing schedule, swiftly reworking parts of *The Town and the City* assisted by Robert Giroux.

The Town and the City traces the fortunes of the Martin family from 1935 to 1946, a period spanning the thirties' Depression, World War Two and its immediate aftermath. The Martin family is large: the father and mother (George and Marguerite) have eight children. In 1935 the eldest, Rose, is 21, Ruth is 18, Joe 17, Francis 15 (his twin Julian died when still 'little'), Peter 13, Elizabeth 12, Charley 9 and Mickey 6. By the end of the novel these children are slightly over ten years older, except Charley (killed in Okinawa during World War Two), and are gathered together to bury George. The novel's focus falls on just three of the children, Joe, Francis, and especially Peter. The fortunes of the mother and father are also given in some detail (for Kerouac, George was the '"greatest hero"' of the novel).[25]

The Martin children live in a Massachusetts mill town on the Merrimac River called Galloway (modeled on Kerouac's home town, Lowell). Initially the focus shifts unevenly from one child to another: Joe becomes increasingly foot-loose, Francis more serious and intellectual, and Peter an athlete honing his prowess. The fates of the females are more thinly sketched: for example, one can sum up the life of the eldest, 'Big Rosie' as a stereotypical one, devoted firstly to helping her mother bring up the large family, and then to a career in nursing.

Gradually the boys leave home. Joe for a while becomes a Jack London-style hobo. Francis goes off to college, eventually ending up at Harvard. Peter wins a sports scholarship to a prep school, and then to university in Philadelphia. From Harvard and Philadelphia Francis and Peter separately gravitate to New York City, which also brings them back into contact with their parents. George and Marguerite's fortunes have gone into decline after George allowed his printing business to run down whilst drinking and gambling. He loses his business and starts work for another printer. These changes cause George and Marguerite to move to New York, where they can both get jobs. The latter part of the novel therefore focuses on the experiences of the various members of the Martin family as they congregate in New York.

The family's fortunes now take a sharp turn because of Pearl Harbor and the onset of war. This cataclysm effects the whole family. Joe enlists first, followed by Rose, who joins an army hospital; Ruth joins the Women's Army Corps; Charley joins the army (eventually dying in combat). However, the impact of the war on Francis and Peter is more complex. Francis, having failed to obtain a commission, is enlisted and sent to boot camp. There, he cannot stomach the discipline and feigns madness in order to get a discharge. Peter, enthusiastic to join the war effort, is still too young, so he instead joins the merchant marine. His participation in the war takes the form of a series of dangerous Atlantic voyages. It is these wartime disruptions that precipitate both Peter's and Francis' moves to New York. Francis joins New York's bohemia, though keeping slightly to its periphery. Peter, too, moves amongst a new circle of friends, also from the bohemian underworld. But Peter's bohemians are less exclusively intellectual, and his loose circle of acquaintances also encompasses an overlapping world of hoodlums and junkies. What the term 'bohemian' embraces is portrayed as opening up in the wake of the war.

These unconventional lifestyles alienate both Francis and Peter from their parents, particularly George. Francis begins to shun his family because they do not fit into his circle, whilst George cannot come to terms with Peter's motley friends. The novel traces the resulting tensions, as well as portraying New York life in the mid-forties. To some extent, their father's death brings the Martin family back together again; but the novel ends with Peter hitching West in the rain, towards an unspecified destination.

The Town and the City, Kerouac's first published novel, is a naturalistic apprentice-work, fitting quite comfortably into a tradition of US writing that prominently features Theodore Dreiser, Jack London, John Steinbeck and Thomas Wolfe. It shares a number of features with this tradition. The Martin family's lives are at first deeply influenced by the Depression and World War Two, and they, like their society, finally face up to an uncertain future in a changed society at a particular historical moment: the commencement of the post-war period. But, alongside this sense that external events shape lives, a parallel emphasis on individuals as having control over their lives also exists. Peter at several points makes self-reliant decisions that change the course of his life, most notably: to walk away from his football scholarship, to enlist in the merchant marines, and to continue to cultivate the friendship of junkies and hoodlums in New York.

This stress on self-cultivation is twined with a plangent romanticism, promoting an image of an ideal America towards which the Martins yearn: 'something strange, something exultant, something that came to him from the scene outside the window where the sun had just appeared on the gray horizon and was spreading a cold rose light over the snowy fields and lonely farmhouses and over the forests of ragged birch that were everywhere slowly turning away from the sweep of the train's progress, all of it remote and beautiful' (*TC*, 146).

This is the same sort of romantic plangency as that found in Wolfe, and Kerouac's novel shares its underlying structure with Wolfe's *Of Time and the River*. Both establish a very traditional distinction between rural town life and city life. But, as well as sharing Wolfe's mistrust of city life, Kerouac's novel also *celebrates* the city—the 'swoop' of Brooklyn bridge, the 'towering' height of Manhattan (*TC*, 345). The city emerges not so much as evil and alienating as shaped by its people and their attitudes. *The Town and the City* sets up a dialogue between depicting the massive impersonality of the city on the one hand and conveying its excitement and potential on the other. The result is an unstable mix of criticism and celebration. The novel portrays New York as on the point of change, full of people in transit: Joe's hobo friends, military personnel and people between jobs. It holds a footloose, shifting work force seeking well-paid war work and, finally, post-war employment. Perhaps most tellingly of all, this transient group of young people includes a cohort of 'girls in America who flit from city to city in search of something they hope to find and never even name ... brusque, businesslike, ebullient, wild, passionate' (*TC*, 449).

Kerouac shows an acute sensitivity to a New York in flux. This is matched by the way this final part of the book is written in a different style: romantic effusiveness largely gives way to a more matter-of-fact, urban style (influenced late on by the letters of Cassady and the prose of Burroughs). The seeds exist here for Kerouac's engagement with a beat generation, as he will call it, and the search for a style to treat with it. *The Town and the City* may be overall an uneven work, but it takes off dramatically in its closing sections.

Following *The Town and the City*'s acceptance, and alongside gearing up to carry out its revisions, Kerouac intensified his search for a form to contain the writing for *On the Road*. What Kerouac now regarded as his next novel evolved at this time into 'an allegory about the betrayal of America'.[26] Much time was spent working on the narrative patterns of what was becoming an increasingly religious work. In a period of his life marked by reading more of Dostoyevsky, and a growing mysticism stimulated by recurrent nightmares about a shrouded traveler, Kerouac also began to see 'the truth' as 'ungraspable', and contingent upon the 'moment'.[27] The aesthetic problem was how to reconcile the elaborate narrative patterning of early drafts of *On the Road* with this new stress upon the immediate 'moment'.

The publisher's advance for *The Town and the City* also generated wild, alcohol-soaked sprees and ambitious plans—one of these resulting in moving with his mother, his sister and her husband to Denver in 1949. When they got there, Kerouac set about reading or re-reading Dostoyevsky, Céline, Alain-Fournier, Spenser, Matthew Arnold, and Keats. Robert Giroux, his editor, also joined him in Denver, and together they worked on *The Town and the City*'s revision. The novel had to be massively whittled down from over one thousand pages, at the publisher's insistence.

Denver, however, did not work out. Mémêre chose to move back to New York (to Richmond Hill). Soon after she left, Kerouac, urged on by a letter from Cassady, traveled to San Francisco to join him (as retold in ***On the Road***; ***Visions of Cody***). Almost immediately, Neal resolved to leave Carolyn (with whom he was re-united) and travel east with Jack. They journeyed through Sacramento, Denver, Chicago, Grosse Pointe (to visit Kerouac's old flame, Edie Parker)—in what was by now the usual hectic, detour-littered adventure across America, ending at Jack's mother's house in Richmond Hill, New York, near Ozone Park. In New York, Neal soon struck up another destructive, child-bearing relationship—with Diana Hansen—whilst Kerouac re-entered the Bohemian literary life and met a woman with whom he formed a semi-stable accommodation, Sara Yokeley. The revisions to *The Town and the City* reached their conclusion at this time. Kerouac also worked more upon *On the Road*, seeking a form 'somewhere between the drama and the Cervantes-novel' for his writing.[28] Out of prison, Ginsberg worked with Kerouac on a jointly written poem, 'Pull My Daisy' (published in Jay Landesman's *Neurotica*, in its Spring 1950 issue, as 'Fie My Fum').

Kerouac was just beginning to attract a small amount of media attention, both immediately prior to *The Town and the City*'s publication and afterwards, when the novel was launched in March 1950 to a mixed critical reception. The book's publication propelled Kerouac on a round of publicity activities which he disliked and handled poorly. The novel sold poorly, too, following mixed, generally unfavorable reviews. Kerouac blamed Giroux, and acquired a deep mistrust of editing.

The cover design for the first edition of Kerouac's *The Town and the City* (1905); its relative conservatism is indicative of this first novel's characteristics.

Eventually, after much celebratory partying, Kerouac left New York for Denver once more, in May 1950, ostensibly to help promote his novel, but chiefly to rejoin Ed White's Denver crowd. His periodic depressions were now occurring more frequently. Beverley Burford, an old Denver flame, did something to dispel these, but at this point Neal Cassady arrived, proposing a trip to Mexico so he could obtain a divorce from Carolyn to enable him to marry Diana Hansen. In Denver, Cassady felt he was treated like a '"white nigger"',[29] and he and Kerouac left quickly, accompanied by Frank Jeffries. In Mexico they met up with Burroughs, but Neal, alleging he had obtained his divorce, quickly returned to New York, deserting a dysentery-stricken Kerouac (as retold in ***On the Road***; ***Visions of Cody***).

In Mexico City, living with Burroughs, Kerouac sought to 'fish as deep as possible into my own subconscious' and not 'just spin silly tales for money'.[30] Heavy marijuana consumption was the method he chose to assist such an exploration. His writing, however, consisted only of some 'jabberwockyish' fairy tales[31] and a failed attempt to fuse parts of *Doctor Sax* with pieces of draft material taken from *On the*

Road. However, he also planned a 'buddy' novel, based on Don Quixote and Sancho Panza, and had a vision of a 'Great Walking Saint of On the Road ... an involuntary pilgrim'.[32] Seeds of *On the Road* can be detected in these churning ideas.

At this point, witnessing the cruelty of Mexican bullfighting precipitated Kerouac's return to New York and some more unhappy heterosexual liaisons; Cassady meanwhile quickly left NYC to return to Carolyn. Kerouac turned back to yet more reading (Melville, Gogol, Shakespeare) and attempted to pull together *On the Road*, including one version from the viewpoint of a young African American (much later reworked to become a core part of *Pic*). He also began meticulous work on a new book, treating with the childhood of himself and Neal Cassady—starting with Neal's early Denver days and drawing, in pastiche, upon Cassady's own prose in his unfinished autobiography, *The First Third*. Early sections of *Visions of Cody* are based on this writing—in particular the depiction of an informal, spontaneous football game.

In September 1950 he composed a novel in French, *La Vie Est Ma Femme* (which remained unpublished). At about this time, however—the Autumn of 1950—a number of Kerouac's friends were in decline, especially Cannastra who was drinking too heavily. After one drunken binge, Cannastra was killed while leaning out of a subway carriage, in an accident that shocked them all. Kerouac met up with Cannastra's bereaved girlfriend, Joan Haverty, and they quickly married in November 1950.

Kerouac's writing at this time was turning sharply towards stylistic experimentation, including imitations of eighteenth-century English writers, endeavors to create a modern version of Proust's style, and attempts to reproduce as conversations the interweave of jazz trios. Just at this time, in December 1950, a long letter (around 13,000 words long) from Cassady arrived. This became known as the 'Joan Anderson letter' and, like Cassady's earlier 'great sex letter', it had an enormous impact on Kerouac. Joan Haverty witnessed its impact: 'Jack picked it up from the front steps and had the opportunity to read it on the subway on his way into town but that wasn't enough. He spent two more hours perusing it in a cafeteria and didn't get home until 6:00'.[33] Kerouac felt it 'ranked among the best things ever written in America ... gather[ing] together the best styles of ... Joyce, Céline, Dosty and Proust ... in the muscular rush of your own narrative style &

excitement'.[34] In letters back to Cassady, Kerouac began to practice this 'muscular rush' in prose,[35] trying to seek out as much immediacy of reminiscence as possible. What Cassady's style offered Kerouac was a model for a type of non-fictional, confessional writing that could be carried across into fiction, to constitute a new type of non-fiction novel, founded upon a directness of style matching exactly the uncensored directness of the subject-matter. The art that Kerouac brought to his adaptation of Cassady's letter-writing style was to make his own editing processes hardly visible, so that, on the surface, his prose reads with the same raw clarity achieved by the very best segments of Cassady's letter. The parts of Cassady's letter that survive, published years later in *The First Third*, are not of consistent merit. However, at its best his Joan Anderson letter offers a direct 'eyeball view ... case history' writing style. At these moments it is plain what excited and influenced Kerouac:[36]

> ... she was white; all white, unless beneath the covers ... was still hidden a speck of pink. The thin ivory arms tapered inward until they reached the slight outward bulge of narrow palms, and the hands in turn bent inward with a more sharp taper only to quickly end in long fingers curled to a point. These things, and her head, with its completely matted hair so black and contrasting with all the whiteness, were the only parts of her visible. Quite normal, I know, but I just couldn't get over how awfully dead she looked. I had so arranged my head above hers that when her eyes opened, after about ten minutes, they were in direct line with mine; they showed no surprise, nor changed their position in the slightest.[37]

The occasional stylistic or syntactical naïveté ('a more sharp taper'), the simple, direct yet precise language, the basic adjectives (white, pink, ivory, narrow, sharp, long, matted, black) and the clearly defined demotic conversationality ('Quite normal, I know, but ...')—it was these qualities of Cassady's writing that attracted Kerouac's enthusiasm, and which he incorporated into his writing, so adding a crucial cutting-edge to his idea that one could, like Cassady, transcribe 'the incidents exactly as they occurred'.[38] His adaptation of Cassady's writing style conjoined with Kerouac's well-established interest in jazz improvisation and 'scat' singing (Kerouac regularly sang 'scat'). All this shows up in his replies to Cassady: a series of letters during December 1950 and January 1951 outlining his major preoccupations (see his *Selected Letters, 1940-1956*); but the Joan Anderson letter from Cassady was to influence even more deeply his approach to fiction writing. As Carolyn Cassady noted, Neal 'enjoyed the challenge of finding words or expressions that described his observations, feelings and impressions in as minute detail as possible. He reveled in the game of continuing a sentence as long as he could before resorting to a period'.[39] Kerouac found this inspirational. He was preparing to move into new territories in this period of stylistic reconsideration, as he evolved his 'spontaneous style ... all first person, fast, mad, confessional ... all detailed'.[40]

Shortly after this, in April 1951, after some false starts, and shut away in Joan Haverty's apartment, he launched upon the rapid typing out of a new version of *On the Road*, on eight twenty-foot strips of tracing paper, taped together to form a continuous roll. The process lasted about twenty days, almost non stop, and consisted of writing prose in a few enormously long paragraphs, with punctuation arranged to maintain the flow.[41] As a sweat-soaked Kerouac typed behind a screen, Haverty passed cups of coffee to him. It seems likely the coffee is what kept Kerouac going, rather than any amphetamine consumption.[42] In Allen Ginsberg's words, the *On the Road* scroll was 'an extraordinary project, sort of a flash of inspiration on a new approach to prose.... An attempt to tell completely, all at once, everything on his mind ... spill it out all at once and follow the convolutions of the active mind for direction'.[43] Though the book was to go through many re-typings and some final pre-publication revisions, the core of *On the Road* was written on this scroll. It drew heavily on Kerouac's four trips across America and his relationship with Neal Cassady on the last three of these trips.

On the Road explores the friendship of two men, Sal Paradise and Dean Moriarty, in the immediate post-war period. It describes their meeting in New York, and then four journeys by Sal: three across America, the last to Mexico. On the first trip Sal hardly sees Dean as he travels from New York to San Francisco and back. The second and third show their friendship at first flowering, then deteriorating as they travel together. On the final excursion, they separate: Dean deserts Sal in Mexico. A muted separation in New York follows.

The novel is structured as a series of adventures 'on the road': Kerouac called it 'an American scene picaresque'.[44] However, a quest motif also exists: Sal comes to regard his friendship with Dean as the key to his search for something he cannot define. He seeks liberation in the long-fabled, mythic frontier West. Yet it remains elusive: when he gets there it seems no longer to exist, except as some 'old rotted covered wagons' next to some 'pool tables sitting in the Nevada desert near a Coca-Cola stand' (150). Indeed, the novel ironically intimates, the long-fabled American Western freedom perhaps never existed. Its promise of release is therefore at best bankrupt. This exposé is invested with an urgency derived from the period when the novel is set. Sal is a World War Two veteran who, just after the end of the war, has split up with his wife and recovered from an illness. In a sense this story of an end to domestic stability (divorce), a period of distress (illness) and a search for a new direction matches the way the USA had emerged from a period of relative isolationism, wrapped in domestic concerns, into reluctant global military engagement followed by a period of as yet ill-defined post-war redefinition. The resulting cultural climate prompts *On the Road*'s reassessment of America and its myths.

Sal's initial quest for a 'pearl' (11) emerges as naïve, and his learning process recasts America's Western myth as a parody: Dean, Sal's 'Western' buddy, is an ambiguous twentieth century 'cowboy'—a car thief rather than a cowpuncher. Sal's narrative is repeatedly ambivalent about Dean. Dean may be 'a side-burned hero of the snowy West' (5) but he is also 'conning me' (7). Sal simply cannot confidently type-cast Dean as hero, though he strives to, and this opens up a 'split' in Sal's response—both to Dean and to the West which Dean represents to Sal. The interplay that results is often presented comically. When Sal reaches the prairie it turns out to be a waste of sagebrush and sand; a girl Sal meets in Cheyenne wants to go East, seeing nothing in the West; and the West itself stands revealed as consisting increasingly of ever-more urbanized communities, like Denver. But Sal is a slow learner, destined in San Francisco to be a 'special policeman', reduced to 'tak[ing] out my gun and play[ing] cowboys in the dark'. Los Angeles turns out to be the 'most brutal of American cities' (64, 85). Sal is always forced back East: his trips in *On the Road* one by one end up becoming 'circular' (78).

Sal simply cannot answer the question, 'Whither goest thou?' (119), which he more or less keeps getting asked. Disillusionment soon dominates: Sal sees he is behaving 'as though I were a traveling salesman' (245). The series of ventures away from and deflated returns to New York becomes a vortex. As he gyrates ever faster, Sal almost desperately comes to apotheosize Dean: at first a 'hero' (5), Dean becomes a 'saint', then an 'Angel' (259), and finally 'God' (285). Sal, deprived of any coherent myth, is increasingly drawn to Dean and his mystical pronouncements upon time and how it might be transfigured. But Dean's attempts to explicate how to transcend time always fail. He can only describe vaguely what he experiences. Finally Dean is reduced to near incoherence: '"Ah, ... so soon, yes. We—we'll know—that is, I don't know. I came on the railroad pass—cabooses—old hard-bench coaches—Texas—played flute and wooden sweet potato all the way"' (307). Faced with this, disengagement from Dean is Sal's almost inevitable response. At the end he leaves Dean, and sweeps off in 'the back of [a] Cadillac', the epitome of America's post-war consumer ethic (309).

Sal's split from Dean typifies 'the story of America. Everybody's doing what they think they're supposed to do' (57). But en route to this ending Sal's position is far from stable. Implicitly or explicitly he looks back on his own behavior with reservations. He recognizes he can be criticized for his desertion of a young Mexican, Terry and her son. Even as Sal wishes, 'I were a Negro ... a Denver Mexican, or even a poor overworked Jap, anything ... but a "white man" disillusioned', this is undercut by a memory of Terry: 'All my life I'd had white ambitions; that was why I'd abandoned ... Terry' (180). In the end, Sal possesses as safety nets people who can help bail him out: a 'rich girl [he] knew', or (most often) his aunt (101). This reminder of social class is duplicated by the way Dean, the ex-reform school car-thief, is excluded from the group of writers and artists amongst whom Sal moves. Given Sal's sensitivities, uncertainty about what attitude to take to Dean results. Dean's sexism is identified (111), but so are its sources: 'Only a guy who's spent five years in jail can go to such ... extremes ... This is the result of years of looking at sexy pictures behind bars ... his bleak impoverishment' (132).

Sal's sense of Dean's social exclusion is matched by his sense of his own somewhat marginalized position, which informs his unsure search for love, his doubts about his sexuality and how this might in turn exclude him. Sal's uncertainties bear within them a contingent sense of how sexuality has become a source of alienation in late-forties' America, saturated by McCarthyesque intolerance. A friend,

Bull, gives voice to the related economic alienation, when offering a critique of built-in obsolescence, 'shelves ... crack ... after six months.... Same with houses, same with clothes.... They prefer making cheap goods so's everybody'll have to go on working and punching timeclocks' (149). Dean later riffs on the same theme: 'they're thinking about ... how much money for gas ... their souls really won't be at peace unless they can latch on to an established and proven worry' (208-9).

To convey all this, *On the Road* modulates between a colloquial American style, and passages where the prose becomes a jazzy ride—sequences of 'spontaneous prose' notating points when Dean and, more rarely, Sal, approach a quasi-mystical 'knowing' of time, which Dean calls the attainment of 'it', or—climactically but unhelpfully—'IT' (306). This seems to be a species of living in the moment that elides, temporarily, the grip of history. Floods of ecstatic recollection are released, but such moments also 'frame' themselves—become their own accuser. Ever-elusive, these moments depend on a momentary mysticism that can only occur through inherently irresponsible escape acts. The sense is that, whilst bourgeois compromises are unsatisfactory, alienation brings with it marginalization, poverty, a dog's life and an inherent selfishness. That he wants his acts to be 'free' is revealed to Sal as paradoxical: the novel's vortex shows that searching for what 'freedom' means in America is always compromised by the fact that it is, in a bitter irony, being sought in a 'land of the free'. To seek to be free is to do what one is 'supposed' to do (57).

Instability results. Firstly, this instability stems from Sal's ambiguous attitude to the class divisions he uncovers in a 'classless' America. Kerouac, in Lucien Carr's words, is 'emotionally aware of class' in this novel.[45] Secondly, it stems from Sal's ambiguity about his sexuality. Thirdly, it stems from a growing uncertainty about authenticity: how can Sal depict 'IT', if 'IT' lies beyond words? These instabilities interact: Sal's doubts concerning authenticity are rooted in his unsureness about his social and sexual identity. Sal's unfinished progress from naïveté reveals that self-knowledge is inescapably elusive within post-war America's predominant intolerance.

Kerouac would much later describe *On the Road* as a 'potboiler',[46] perhaps because it possesses a comparatively straightforward narrative structure and Sal Paradise does not quite display the same degree of divided self-knowledge that

Kerouac's later narrators possess. But the book is in fact a sophisticated exploration of how post-war American youth sought to reassess what it meant to be American. To this extent it has to be recognized that what finally reached publication in 1957 was very much more mediated than the 1951 scroll version, which offers more immediacy.

This marathon effort became known as the scroll version of *On the Road*, finally published in 2007. It was, in important ways, very different from the version published in 1957 which went through many years of editing, re-editing, additional writing and re-writing. Most strikingly, the 1951 scroll does not use pseudonyms, other than rarely and inconsistently. It is also more immediate and, at points, much franker.

Soon after this, Mémêre moved to Kerouac's sister's in Kinston, North Carolina, whilst Neal visited the Kerouacs' apartment, and urged Joan and Jack to come to San Francisco (as retold in ***On the Road***; ***Visions of Cody***). Kerouac was open to this suggestion and eventually acted on it because—yet again—things were not going smoothly in his relationship: Kerouac and Joan Haverty had moved out of his mother's house since his over-close relationship to his mother threatened to disrupt his marriage. But the switch to Joan's apartment did not work. His separation from Joan occurred just before *On the Road* was completely typed out in May 1951. Consequently, the scroll had to be finished off in Lucien Carr's apartment. There, famously, Carr's dog, Potchky, chewed off the scroll's end, which had to be recomposed later. This new ending shows clear signs of how Kerouac's later editing made the novel less hard-hitting: Sal's narrative in the published 1957 version finally dissolves into sentimental nostalgia—heavily influenced by Thomas Wolfe and drawing upon an exchange with one of Neal Cassady's children in 1954. In *Some of the Dharma*, Kerouac notes a conversation he had with Neal and Caroline Cassady's children:

> "Why is the mountain sitting there?" (man asks children)
> Jamie: "Because nobody's on there and we're not supposed to climb on it because the dirt'll fall off."
> "Who made the mountain?" (man)
> They: "God made it."
> Man: "Who is God?"
> Cathy: "Us." And right then Cathy sayd: "He wants to play with the fence."

> Man: "Who?"
> Cathy: (showing Bear toy) "Me. Dont you know that I am Poo Bear?"
> God is Poo Bear. (*SD*, 17-18)

This conversation took place in February 1954, when Kerouac was staying with the Cassadys in San Jose. In a May 1954 letter to Carolyn Cassady, after Jack had returned to the east coast, he wrote: 'Let me know about the little ones who know that God is Pooh-Bear'.[47] If Kerouac came to think of God as Poo[h] Bear" after talking to the Cassady's children, as seems likely, then the idea would not have been part of the 1951 scroll version of *On the Road*, but only added to the manuscript at least three years later. The 1951 version could not have ended like this:

> ... don't you know that God is Pooh Bear? The evening star must be drooping and shedding her sparkler dims on the prairie, which is just before the coming of complete night that blesses the earth, darkens all rivers, cups the peaks and folds the final shore in, and nobody, nobody knows what's going to happen to anybody besides the forlorn rags of growing old, I think of Dean Moriarty, I even think of old Dean Moriarty, the father we never found, I think of Dean Moriarty. (*OR*, 309-310)

The plangent tone of this passage differs from the tone of the scroll typescript, which is far more direct and descriptive—and often a better read.

Excited by *On the Road*'s completion, Kerouac wanted the scroll published as a book as soon as possible. But he immediately encountered a problem. Rushing into the office of Robert Giroux, who he hoped would take the book, he unrolled the 120 feet scroll in high excitement. Giroux's reaction was sensibly to ask how such a typescript could possibly be revised. Since Kerouac's evolving philosophy of writing had come to be broadly opposed to any rewriting, he left Giroux's office almost immediately. Other publishers, when approached, also saw problems with the text's experimentalism. This setback was matched by one in Kerouac's private life: he definitively broke up with Joan (just after she realized she was pregnant—with Jan, whom Kerouac always refused to recognize), a development marked by a move back to Kinston to rejoin Mémêre. There, worn down, he accepted on reflection the need to revise *On the Road* and preliminarily retyped it on bond, clearly dividing the novel into five sections. The dilution of the 'muscular rush' of the scroll version of the novel had commenced: the typescript was now amenable to revision. It seems quite probable that later, when Kerouac returned to earlier versions of *On the Road* in order to put together a final version, it was to this retyping that he turned. For Ginsberg, the constant revisions that developed represented a substantial loss: 'The original mad version is greater than the published [1957] version .... a magnificent single paragraph several blocks long, rolling like the road itself'. Ginsberg forecast that 'when everybody's dead' the scroll version 'would be published as it is'—and he was to be proved correct, for it was only finally released in 2007, when almost everyone was indeed dead.[48]

Chapter Three: From *Doctor Sax* to *Maggie Cassidy*

Having finished retyping the scroll version of *On the Road*, Kerouac immediately began to envision another book dealing with Neal Cassady, surrounding him with such characters as an African-American child called Pic (a further seed for *Pic*). He also planned a new jazz novel, 'Horn', and again read extensively (Faulkner, Flaubert, Hawthorne, Henry James, Gorky, D.H. Lawrence, Blake, Melville, Whitman, Emily Dickinson, Hart Crane, Carl Sandburg, W.B. Yeats, and yet more Proust). Despite falling ill with phlebitis again, which caused acute pain in his legs, Kerouac continued revising *On the Road*. As his health improved he visited New York, and on one occasion watched his artist friend, Ed White 'sketching' in architectural notebooks. White suggested he try such outline sketching 'with words',[49] and for a period after this Kerouac explored this approach (the opening pages of *Visions of Cody* contains some of the resulting sketchings). On another 1951 New York visit, he met Gregory Corso. However, pressing invites from Cassady to join him in San Francisco, the chance of shipping out on a merchantman with Cru from San Pedro, and maintenance demands from Joan drove him to the West Coast.

On arrival on the West Coast Kerouac failed to get signed on as a member of Cru's ship (as retold in **'Piers of the Homeless Night'**, in ***Lonesome Traveler***), so instead he took up residence with the Cassadys, taking a job on the railroad in order to save up to travel back to Mexico. He also recorded himself reading out a version of *Doctor Sax* on one of the very first mass-produced, commercially-sold tape machines. And, at Cassady's instigation, he had an affair with Carolyn, proving to be, for her, a poor lover. Yet the ménage-à-trois worked, if rather precariously, and during 1952 Kerouac and Cassady (alone or along with visitors to the house) also held tape-recording sessions, transcribing the tapes to read back the next day (*Visions of Cody* incorporates some of these transcription 'loops'). Kerouac also witnessed the filming of Joan Crawford in *Sudden Fear* in the streets of San Francisco (see ***Visions of Cody***), and worked this episode into an ever-burgeoning revision of *On the Road*. This episode, along with other writings carried out in this period and intended for *On the Road*, eventually separated out to become a highly experimental and disconcerting collage of pieces of more or less separate yet inter-related writings. So his account of the filming of *Sudden Fear* turns up as an episode called 'Joan Rawshanks' not in *On the Road*, but in this separate collage-work, which eventually assumed the shape of *Visions of Cody*. This cross-semination explains why Kerouac speaks of *On the Road* at about this time as being 'like *Ulysses*':[50] he is referring not to the core narrative of his adventures with Neal Cassady, found in the slightly more conservatively structured *On the Road*, but to writing experiments revolving around the tape transcripts of his nights with Cassady, some of which would be included verbatim in *Visions of Cody*.

Kerouac also frequently visited jazz clubs and experimented with peyote with Philip Lamantia. He was at this time in high creative flood as a writer but negotiations with Carl Solomon, a representative for Ace Books, a potential publisher for *On the Road*, became, in Nicosia's words, a 'tragedy of errors'.[51] When Solomon 'accepted' *On the Road* for Ace in January 1952 he probably thought he was accepting a revision of the already legendary 1951 scroll version. The work Kerouac was in fact talking about to Solomon was not a revision of the original typescript roll but a prolix inter-cutting of many different layers of 'road' experimentation. It was a total revamp—one that would largely consist of the experimentation which ended up in *Visions of Cody*. Kerouac was assembling what was effectively an entirely new book, incorporating 'sketching', increasingly ambitious and fraught searches for spontaneity, and the San Francisco tape transcripts—a highly experimental work rooted in 'wild form'.[52] The correspondence shows Kerouac planning to finish this experimentally oriented *On the Road* quickly, and turning back to *Doctor Sax*.

What exactly was going on at this time, as *On the Road* was constantly revised and expanded, is therefore difficult to disentangle. When it became apparent to Kerouac that Ace Books probably would not accept the sort of extended, 'wild' version of the novel that was evolving, preferring something shorter, he rapidly typed out a new, compact, quickfire version of the road travels of Dean and Sal—or, Cody and

Duluoz—to offer to Ace Books as a kind of pulp paperback version. Kerouac also notified Ace that he would later submit a whole new, very much larger, typescript for hardback publication. Perhaps at this point he realized that *On the Road* in its 1951 scroll form was something entirely different to the long, typescript, lacing together of different narrative experiments that he first thought he might send to Ace. Ace anyway never committed to either the quickfire or the much longer version of *On the Road*, perhaps partly put off by Ginsberg's simultaneous attempts to get Ace to publish Cassady's writings—similar as these were to some of Kerouac's work. However, the picture began to clear when Kerouac recognized that what might be called his proto-*Visions of Cody*—a complete recasting of and copious experimental elaboration of 'On the Road'—was so different and extraordinary that it could never be grafted onto the scroll-based *On the Road* narrative. They simply did not go together. Two very different works began to separate out.

Accordingly in April 1952 Kerouac probably offered Ace what was later to become the closing pages of *Visions of Cody* (*VC*, 338-398), which read like a speeded-up and experimental rewrite of the scroll manuscript This benzedrine-laced version of Kerouac's adventures on the road with Cassady recapitulated much of *On the Road* but with less restraint than either the 1951 version or the final 1957 book. It is worth reading this closing section of *Visions* alongside the scroll version and the much-edited 1957 version of *On the Road*. The version in *Visions* is the most experimental in its narrative style—and the least censored:

> Scroll 1951 [2007]: The fag said he would like nothing better but to know what Neal thought about all this. Warning him first that he had once been a hustler in his youth, Neal proceeded to handle the fag like a woman, tipping him over legs in the air and all and gave him a monstrous huge banging. I was so non-plussed all I could do was sit and stare in my corner. And after all that the fag turned over no money to us, tho he made vague promises for Denver, and on top of that he became extremely sullen and I think suspicious of Neal's final motives. He kept counting his money and checking on his wallet. Neal threw up his hands and gave up. "You see, man, it's better not to bother. Give them what they secretly want and they of course immediately become panic-stricken." (1951 [2007]: 307)
>
> *On the Road* 1957: ... Dean asked him [the fag] how much money he had. I was in the bathroom. The fag became

> extremely sullen and I think suspicious of Dean's final motives, turned over no money and made vague promises for Denver. He kept counting his money and checking on his wallet. Dean threw up his hands and gave up. "You see, man, it's better not to bother. Offer them what they secretly want and they of course immediately become panic-stricken." (209)
>
> *Visions of Cody* c.1952 [1972]: That night the gangbelly broke loose between Cody and the skinny skeleton, sick: Cody thrashed him on rugs in the dark, monstrous huge fuck, Olympian perversities, slambanging big sodomies that made me sick, subsided with him for money; the money never came. He'd treated the boy like a girl! ... I sat in the castrated toilet listening and peeking, at one point Cody has thrown him over legs in the air like a dead hen ... (1972: 358-9)

It is clear how much more mediated and conventional the 1957 version of *On the Road* is, compared to *Visions*' wild form, or even the 1951 scroll's depictions. It seems likely that at about this time in 1952 Kerouac saw the need to separate off the *On the Road* narrative from the wilder experimentation that was eventually assembled in *Visions of Cody*.

At this point Kerouac took advantage of an invitation by Burroughs to join him in Mexico, and so traveled down there. He wrote this trip up as the beginning of a new book about Native Americans (a beginning that developed into 'Mexico Fellaheen',[53] in *Lonesome Traveler*) and then turned back to *Doctor Sax*. The 'wild form' freedom developed during working on *Visions of Cody* now facilitated progress on *Doctor Sax*: it was rapidly completed in Mexico during a period of heavy marijuana use.

Doctor Sax portrays Jacky Duluoz's childhood in late nineteen-twenties and thirties Lowell. Jacky roams Lowell's streets, encountering imaginary adversaries: Doctor Sax, a criminal alchemist, the vampiric Count Condu, and other figures drawn from myth, cartoon and fantasy.[54] These encounters lead Jacky into a series of nightmare adventures. Initially, he regards Sax with fascinated dread but progressively comes to identify him as an ally, assisting him in the tracking down of a more potent and dangerous phantom-enemy, a giant snake. The narrative climaxes in a confrontation with this evil snake, in front of which Jacky and Sax are powerless. But an ambiguous victory is delivered by a large bird, which swoops down from the sky and bears the snake away.

Such a summary suggests the novel has a clear structure. The experience of reading it is, however, quite different since it is written experimentally, using what Kerouac called '*wild form*'[55]—an approach related to that used in parts of *Visions of Cody*'s elaborations upon *On the Road*. In this instance, Kerouac develops a style in *Doctor Sax* to facilitate the interfusion of dream and reality (indebted to Burroughs' factualism). Even *Doctor Sax*'s opening series of vivid memory-sketches, creating a multi-faceted portrait of Lowell, are written with a dream-like, rhythmic repetitiveness. This intermingling of fantasy and reality leads on to Book Two which begins by depicting Jacky inventing a game with marbles to create a fantasy horse race so meticulously realized that the boy almost feels it is real. This solitary, escapist game is set beside a 'sketch' of Jacky's father working as a pool-hall manager, underlining how, in turn, the adult-world produces its own escapist entertainments. Book Three abruptly crosses over from this inter-lacing of dream-and-reality into a totally imaginary world, set in a ruined castle above Lowell where the snake lurks, along with vampiric specters haunting Jacky. Book Four extends this procedure: a Lowell of dream-and-reality and an imaginary Lowell alternate. This time, however, the imaginary Lowell becomes the creation of young Jacky Duluoz (writing as 'Doctor Sax')—it is his juvenile attempt at writing a fantasy-story, about a deadly attack by Sax on a 'jazz-age' party. This is interwoven (again) with a real memory—of a man dying on Lowell's bridge across the Merrimac. Book Five details a flood on this river, which stimulates further literary efforts by Jacky (some poetry) but also unleashes a final flood of the imagination—namely, Book Six, 'The Castle'. This closing section is wholly a fantasy adventure, as a huge snake, bearing down on Lowell, is snatched away by a giant bird. Progressively, fantasy takes over the narrative until finally, in a startling climax, all the fantasy-protagonists disappear or change—in Sax's case, into an ordinary working man, wearing a working man's clothing.

Doctor Sax thus explores the way that, in boyhood, memory and fantasy can interfuse. As a recreation of childhood, like most such recreations, it is laced by nostalgia. This is particularly potent because of the period in which it is set, 1927-1936, and the community Jacky remembers growing up within: a predominantly working-class French-Canadian neighborhood in Lowell, where most employment came from the Depression-hit mills on the Merrimac. It is represented as an economically beleaguered, tight-knit, somewhat closed community in decline, dominated by a shared language (joual) and a shared religion (Catholicism), which together form the backbone of the banter and gossip in the streets and yards of French-Canadian Lowell. But the incipient nostalgia is mollified by a recognition that this is also a community in transition—moving from slow decay into 1930s' disintegration.

Doctor Sax is also, however, a portrait of a young French-Canadian American's growth from childhood through puberty into adolescence; John Clellon Holmes called it, 'probably the best book about adolescence ... since *Huck Finn*'.[56] The blurring of the division between memory and dream as they become 'intermixed' (5), explores a sexual coming-of-age. So the geography of Lowell is laid out as a dream/memory landscape, within which the narrator and his childhood friends stand at a turning point described as a corner or 'doorway' (52) to which the story constantly returns. This threshold space is in large part the one dividing the boy, Jacky, from the adolescent, the pre-pubescent from the pubescent. The entrance of dream into the narrative is crucial, clarifying how the story operates in part as a set of puberty fantasies.

The child's relationship with Doctor Sax dramatizes these fantasies. Sax is a character from the child's puberty-dreams—an amalgam of Jacky's own fantasies and the escapist fantasy-hero 'adult' models fictionalized in his reading of cheap comic-books: *The Shadow Magazine*, *Star Western* and *Pistol Pete*.[57] Doctor Sax surveys the boys at night—playing, reading, sleeping and dreaming: 'Doctor Sax is hiding in the darkroom ... in that darkness coming from behind the door' (*DS*, 68). Progressively the boys' activities, under Sax's surveillance, come to revolve around the Merrimac River, which is recurrently represented as ominous, swollen and raging. The river, like Sax, is a source of mystery and threat, its swelling and power resonantly phallic.

But the adolescent's erections are too disturbing to be simply contained by one fantasy-monster. Sax, paradoxically, becomes increasingly a source of reassurance, protecting Jacky from a giant, threatening snake, lurking in the cellarage of a dreamy recreation of a Castle. Here, also, Jacky's 'vampire', Count Condu, lives. These dangerous encounters charge the boyhood fantasy with overtly erotic imagery, through which it becomes clear that the mysterious ambiguity of Doctor Sax is to be preferred to the more ominous, rising threats posed by Condu and the Snake. Jacky has to learn to come to terms with his pre-pubescent erections, marked by a discovery of 'sex'. Increasingly, emphasis falls on Jacky's masturbatory activities until, finally, in Book Six, symbolically in the aftermath of a huge flood, Jacky brings his masturbation attempts to full orgasm, depicted as the unleashing of the snake upon the world: '*The snake was coming for me*!!'. Orgasm finally achieved, Jacky is left 'sat on the ground completely stunned, legs spread', whilst a huge bird carries the snake/erection away, surrounded by a sperm-like flock of 'white Doves' (241-42). Doctor Sax is relegated to being a childhood dream.

Heavily drug-influenced (mostly marijuana), *Doctor Sax* is a haunting vision of 1920s' and 1930s' childhood. Written from the perspective of the 1950s—a period of affluence and increased explicitness about child sexuality—it looks back to a more repressed yet also compact and so somehow more magical community—pre-war, French-Canadian Lowell. Whilst the omnipresence of poverty and pollution is recognized, the innocent intensity fostered there is nostalgically recalled, with its joual, and Catholic rituals. The sense is that while there may have been gains, much is lost in the transition from the pre- to the post-war in America.

At this time, Kerouac moved into a period of sustained drug experimentation and general dissipation. He tried peyote alongside his marijuana-use, and enjoyed cheap Mexican child prostitutes. He was still contemplating a jazz-based novel, but hearing of Clellon Holmes's proto-plans for his jazz novel, *The Horn*, he reacted with paranoia, a reaction exacerbated by Solomon's (and Ginsberg's) rejection of *Visions of Cody*.

These ructions and Kerouac's freeloading also promoted a rift with Burroughs and a return to his sister in North Carolina (Rocky Mount). There he put the finishing touches to *Doctor Sax* before launching out on a brief substance-abusing excursion into New York. At the same time he was resolving to rejoin Neal and Carolyn in California, and traveled there via Denver (in 1952). In San Jose he made some more tapes of himself and Neal talking (see ***Visions of Cody***), read sections of *Doctor Sax* into the tape machine, and began working on the Southern Pacific Railroad. However, after a brief Indian Summer the ménage with Carolyn and Neal finally disintegrated, and Jack hit Skid Row, San Francisco. At this time he was still struggling to get books published: besides *On the Road* itself, there was *Doctor Sax* and *Visions of Cody*, now consistently conceived of as distinct from *On the Road*.

Visions of Cody is a highly experimental assault: throughout, Kerouac simultaneously tries to capture authenticity whilst also attacking the very idea. Trying to deliver 'the complete Cody' to the reader (36) dooms the book's writer and narrator, Duluoz (Kerouac), to failure. The book traces the failure of different attempts to achieve this aim of delivering Cody (Cassady) completely. In this sense, *Visions of Cody* is designed to fail.

The book opens with short sketches of the sights and smells of the post-war American urban experience. Basic bodily needs and functions are depicted, and the focus falls on food-joints, railway stations and other glimpses of the city. Evocative, *hungry* descriptions of food add to the general sense of poverty pervading these early pages, drawing on the perspective of the poor. The narrative, like Jack, roams decaying downtown streets. Cody at first is mentioned only in passing, as Jack's 'visions' of New York are impressionistically sketched. But gradually the descriptions recede, Jack's memory grows dominant, and his narrative admits more thoughts of Cody. The book's focus shifts more to the recapturing of long-forgotten memories: Jack recalls his father, his family, his family's house (25-27). As these in turn become interwoven with dreams, the origins of Jack's perspective on Cody are established. Only then is the voice of Cody himself reproduced: an actual letter Cassady ('Cody') wrote to Kerouac is included.

Part Two begins with an account of Cody's youth (matching that of Jack's), revolving around the days when Cody hung around Denver pool halls as an adolescent. But again the narrative becomes progressively more complex. The account of Cody's youth is increasingly interwoven with later memories of Jack spending time with Cody. Finally, memories of Jack's own recent past appear. The way Jack's past shapes his visions of Cody are further clarified. Jack's authentic version of Cody will be, precisely, only *Jack's* version. All this serves as a prologue to the '*visions*' yet to come.

Indeed, Part Three is the first full attempt to render a 'vision' of Cody—specifically, of his voice, caught during five days of audio-taped conversations. These are transcribed in full in an attempt to capture Duluoz's questions to Cody about his memories of his past, and Cody's replies. The transcripts are rambling and seem inconsequential, other than as records of how Duluoz (Kerouac) interacts with Cody (Cassady). But the tape of the fourth night clearly offers some 'visions', firstly of Cody's relationship to his father, during which Cody reads out a letter from his father, and secondly of a series of New York adventures by Jack and Cody, during which the two young men's paths come ever closer together and start crossing.

The tapes are apparently unedited, but it becomes plain that editorial control is inevitably being exercised. Explanations need to be inserted because of taping problems or to provide other contextual information. The tapes themselves also increasingly debate issues of authenticity: how to convey 'what *really* happened' (205) and whether it is possible not to '*lie*' (218). The tapes start to revolve around the problem of memory's reliability. But, above all, the tape transcripts detail Cody's reflections on the difficulties of *verbalizing* experience and the problem of transcribing these verbalizations. How one *can* truly envision is the implicit question.

The next section, 'Imitation of the Tape', elaborately reworks both the tapes' and the book's central themes in a variety of literary styles, each striving to provide a way of compellingly conveying authentic insight. The writing styles of Shakespeare, Whitman, Melville, Proust, Stein, Hemingway, Steinbeck, Henry Miller, Faulkner, Joyce and Wolfe are all tested in this way. Each variation transforms Jack's memories, descriptions, dreams and fantasies differently. These imitations of great literary stylists are interwoven with pastiches of Ginsberg and Burroughs. Organized into a 'running consciousness stream' (258), they are the voices ringing in Jack's head. Normal reading strategies just won't work in this section, as it gets ever wilder. A 'burlesk show' is instead created, in which 'you can get high as you want' (266). So, for example, imitations of Faulkner and Joyce are set alongside parodies of popular cultural styles: comic books, cartoons, comedians' routines (W.C. Fields), jazz lyrics (Billie Holliday), TV (the Flintstones), sport commentaries, movie reviews: 'Ernest Hummingbird ... with bottle of gin and bananas, goes off laughing in the night ... descendant of the caveman who made his wife a gore' (266). Distinctions between 'high' and 'low' art dissolve in a 'happy moment of junctures' (272) defying analysis. Jack is searching for a way to turn the raw tape transcripts into meaningful 'art'. But the sense is that all this will end inconclusively. What *can* conceivably constitute 'authentic art' instead becomes the central question as the book becomes a text full of copies and simulacra, increasingly mistrustful of its own narrative projects. No narrative or literary style seems able to communicate *vision* any better than the 'exactly' transcribed ramblings of Jack and Cody.

The next section, 'Joan Rawshanks in the Fog', re-explores such issues from a different angle. It consists of an account of the shooting of a Joan Crawford film, *Sudden Fear*, on location in the streets of San Francisco, and how in the process the director controls the film star and the production company controls the audience. It focuses on the way cinema is never just a reproduction, with the camera never lying, but always artifice, *contriving* to reproduce reality. At one point, the film director instructs Joan not to cry but to look fearful, and Duluoz asks: 'doesn't it seem as though the script would have been materially altered on the point of this decision' (279). This also explains why 'Joan Rawshanks' is followed by yet another 'Imitation', this time of the masturbation passages in *Ulysses*, reworked to represent Duluoz masturbating over a film-star pin-up (in an oblique reference to Crawford's porn-star past). This post-war American image, rooted in Hollywood's erotic icons, precisely shows how the mind is invaded, if never controlled, by media constructions of desire in America.

Finally the text moves on from these explorative 'imitations' towards its finale, a quickfire account of a number of journeys undertaken by Jack and Cody. Interspersed in this are further imitative parodies of the tape transcripts which drive home the extent to which Kerouac's endless modulations of style are themselves homages, particularly to Joyce's *Ulysses*.[58] These allusions remind us that any version of Jack's and Cody's life on the road is inevitabiy only a literary imitation of reality. Thus, though Jack's and Cody's adventures bear a close similarity to Sal's and Dean's in *On the Road*, they are qualitatively different. The differences between the books' competing accounts underline how what constitutes 'authenticity' is not fixed but always fugitive, changing from moment to moment. It is in this translation/reprise section that the full contradictoriness of Jack's feelings towards Cody become apparent: the recognition of Cody's selfishness, egotism and self-centeredness is entwined with admiration for his enthusiastic energy, in a complex mare's nest of love and hate: 'he's an angel .... /But enough of my greatest enemy—because while I saw him as an angel, a god, etcetera, I also saw him as a devil, an old witch, even an old bitch from the start' (298).

As this summary makes clear, *Visions of Cody*'s structure is highly complex. One has to negotiate its shape-shifting however one can. Overall, the text operates as a series of endless modulations on the subject of Cody, bonded together by certain recurring motifs—for example, the color brown, which stands for an ambiguous mixture of holiness, poverty and decay within the urban, and red neon, the color of advertising display, alluring yet dangerous in its designs. The book becomes both an impressive, if dauntingly difficult, reflection on the impossibility of writing ever rendering truly a *vision* of life and a celebration of the endless resources available to the writer when undertaking this futile attempt.

Kerouac had by this time produced a spate of highly experimental writings that one after the other were proving difficult to get published. Yet, despite these unpublished projects, Kerouac still started to plan a new work, which came to center on his Lowell childhood/youth (this became *Maggie Cassidy*), whilst also working full-time on the railroad. Soon he commenced an account of these railroad experiences, 'Wine in the Railroad Earth' (later entitled 'October in the Railroad Earth', and finally, **'The Railroad Earth'**).

However, phlebitis problems caused him to give up his railroad life and he returned to Mexico with Cassady in late 1952. Kerouac linked up again briefly with Burroughs (who, faced with legal difficulties, soon had to leave), then settled down to a creative burst—writing a never-published novelette and more work on his evolving 'Duluoz Legend'. Cassady left Mexico and Kerouac became lonely. After using up $50 sent by John Clellon Holmes from the money Holmes received for his 'Beat Generation' novel, *Go!* (a 1952 work of which Kerouac was jealous and about which he was angry, feeling it had stolen his thunder since *On the Road* remained unpublished), Kerouac headed back to New York. There he read Genet and worked in earnest on *Maggie Cassidy*. The Ace deal over *Road/Cody* having broken down, Viking, encouraged by Malcolm Cowley, was at this time considering *On the Road*, *Doctor Sax* and drafts of early sections of *Maggie Cassidy*. But failure to get anything actually published made Kerouac increasingly frustrated and quarrelsome. He did, however, complete *Maggie Cassidy*.

Maggie Cassidy portrays the love affair of two teenagers living in Lowell: a French-Canadian American, Jacky Duluoz, and the Irish Maggie Cassidy. However, it is a story emphasizing not so much love's eternality as its fleeting precariousness.

Jacky and Maggie meet at a New Year's Eve ball in 1938, and the novel traces the fumbling course of their love. Maggie is one year older than Jacky, and he feels she is exerting pressure on him to bring to their relationship more commitment than he is prepared to offer, whilst herself failing to completely clarify her own level of commitment. At first he pulls away whilst she presses, but progressively the roles become reversed. He draws closer to her, and finally (and a little reluctantly) breaks up with his previous girlfriend, Pauline (Moe) Cole. In contrast, Maggie begins to turn away from him by becoming involved with another man, Roger Rousseau. When Jacky leaves Lowell to attend College on a sports scholarship, these tensions come to a head as Maggie's dream of conventional domesticity clashes with New York's alluring promise of fortune and fame.[59]

Maggie Cassidy is also, however, a story of a tangled love affair laced with issues of class, ethnic identity and prejudice. A constant undercurrent lays stress on the differences in class and ethnic background between Jacky and Maggie, who comes from the wrong side of the river (the equivalent of the wrong side of the tracks). Jacky resists his parents' pressure to stay with Pauline, gradually bringing them round to Maggie. This success can be related to changes in the Lowell community's makeup which was becoming increasingly fluid as employment patterns changed, with textile millwork progressively shrinking (especially during the Depression). What had been strong ethnic and socio-economic divides have weakened, and in a sense Jack's sexual relationships track these changes and the resulting tensions. Lowell is changing and the society becoming more hybrid, as Centralville and even 'Little Canada' in Pawtucketville become more diverse and less segregated. But the novel does not reduce things in any simple way: Jacky's reluctance to face up to his sexuality and then the award of a sports scholarship create a sense of how social and sexual factors always interface within the force-fields of 'love'. The descriptions of Jacky Duluoz's sporting prowess are therefore not a counterpoint to the account of his relationship with Maggie, but integrally bound up in the progress of the affair. The sports scholarship serves as a potential means of levering Jacky out of working-class Lowell life, its drudgery, and the resulting 'sad, crapulous look' of the town (53). But college is itself laced with prejudices. When Maggie visits him she is 'snobbed' by the 'wealthy lavishly gowned girls' (176) and, finally, Jacky returns to Lowell having apparently failed to integrate in New York.

Maggie Cassidy is a powerful study of young adulthood, its ambiguities and uncertainties, and how class, ethnicity and sexuality impact on these in the terrain that is conventionally but simplistically represented as somehow complete in itself: love.

Allen Ginsberg, Photograph of Jack Kerouac, 'East 7th Street at Ave A', New York, Fall 1953.

Kerouac's agent now (in 1953) took *On the Road*, *Cody* and *Sax* to Malcolm Cowley at Viking, who showed interest but wanted too many revisions. So later that year Kerouac returned to his West Coast brakeman's job briefly (**'Railroad Earth'**, in ***Lonesome Traveler***), and then signed on the *SS Carruth*, bound out of San Francisco for Alabama, New York and Korea. However, on-shore misbehavior in Mobile caused him to leave the ship by mutual agreement in New Orleans (see **'Slobs of the Kitchen Sea'**, in ***Lonesome Traveler***).

He returned to Richmond Hill where he made arrangements for Ginsberg to act for him to get a version of the original *On the Road* published, since Cowley was enthusiastic. He also started to revise *On the Road*, now almost stripped of its *Visions of Cody* experimentation, which was substantially replaced by retypings of the 1951 scroll or (at least as often) the 1952 retyped versions.

Kerouac also worked more on 'The Railroad Earth' and read Wilhelm Reich's *The Function of the Orgasm*. Reich, he explained to Ed White, stimulated his interest in seeking orgasmic release in writing, composing 'like orgasm from center of mind and jewel point of interest in memory or vision therein outward like coming ... in one wild impulse surge electric language' in order to 'swirl my brain from commonplace expression into seas of English'.[60] These sentiments contain the seeds of some of the proposals advanced in his famous 1958 'essay' on writing, 'Essentials of Spontaneous Prose'. This essay, along with 'Belief and Technique for Modern Prose' became highly influential by stressing the need to swim outwards from a 'jewel center' image and insisting upon never after-thinking to 'improve' or 'defray' impressions ('Essentials', 72-73). Yet such an emphasis on spontaneity by Kerouac stemmed more from an idealization of his compositional approach than from his actual, more complex practice; 'Essentials' is tainted, ironically, with after-thinking about what he was about in his writing.

Chapter Four: From *The Subterraneans* to 'The Railroad Earth'

Reading Wilhelm Reich not only aroused Kerouac's interest in seeking orgasmic release in his writing, it also stimulated his interest in sexual relationships. He was mixing with some New York jazz-joint aficionados at this time, many of them hard drug users. Amongst them was Alene Lee, an African-American, and Kerouac and she soon began to have an intense affair (as retold in ***The Subterraneans***). He respected her intelligence and sensitivity, even writing to Ed White to say he loved her 'not only as a "woman", but as a "man"'.[61] Apart from its sexist implications, this observation perhaps also signals how his sexual identity at this time was in some turmoil (at about this time, for example, he slept with Gore Vidal). Perhaps this contributed to his relationship with Alene lasting only one month. As Kerouac was drawn back into the ambit of Ginsberg and Burroughs (now back in New York), Gregory Corso, part of their circle, found Alene a magnetic attraction. Kerouac's jealousy, insecurity and uncertainties, especially over his sexuality, and a desire to return to the security of Mémêre's house, brought an end to his relationship with Alene in October 1953 (as retold in ***The Subterraneans***). Almost immediately, he sat down and wrote *The Subterraneans*, in three nights, using benzedrine to keep awake.

The Subterraneans tells the story of a brief, intense love affair. Its narrator, Leo Percepied, a 'Canuck' (i.e., from a poor French-Canadian background) becomes involved with Mardou Fox, half African-American and one quarter Cherokee. He sees her in a bar in San Francisco where she hangs around with a bohemian group of writers, jazz enthusiasts and intellectuals. Mardou has been emotionally damaged by some past relationships within this group and is wary of further entanglements. Leo, however, immediately he sees her, determines to become involved. After a short courtship she goes to bed with him. For a while they enter into a highly charged relationship. However, the affair soon starts to deteriorate, since neither can quite decide what they want from each other. Leo in particular keeps leaving to go back to his mother's house to write. So when a friend of Leo's, Yuri Gligoric, horns in on Mardou, the couple are sufficiently ambivalent about their relationship for her to respond to Yuri's advances. Indeed, Percepied steps deliberately away, creating sufficient space for Yuri's overtures to be accepted. Perversely, however, Percepied then reacts badly to Mardou's infidelity and they break up. The novel traces this process, spanning a period of only a few weeks.

The Subterraneans is cast as a confessional, first-person narrative account of this affair,[62] but as well as offering a searing exposé of the narrator's mixed motives, it is marred by obvious repressions. Percepied can be read as the French for 'pierced-foot' and Leo does indeed constantly limp through this narrative, stumbling over his mixed motivations, betraying both his exploitative approach to heterosexual relationships and an uncertainty concerning his motives in developing his relationship with an African/Native American. When he confesses to experiencing a sense of exotic allure, this carries more than a trace of racism. Like Achilles (and his heel), Leo's maleness actually conceals a fatal flaw. But his lameness also relates him to Oedipus ('swollen foot'), and hence (indirectly) to Freud's 'Oedipus complex'. Indeed, Mardou calls into question his underlying motives in constantly returning to the safety of his mother's house. The result is a powerful sense of a young man fundamentally adrift, quite unable to bring into full consciousness his motives and desires. Leo himself is breaking down: 'Percepied? Who's Percepied?', the narrative asks, 'has he been busted yet?'. A sense is conveyed of the first-person protagonist as close to being 'busted'—fragmented by his circumstances, unable to come fully to terms with or fit into the 'Beach' culture with which he is involved.

In *The Subterraneans* Kerouac perfects the process of accessing memory through particular 'trigger' phrases, 'jewel centers', as he described them, or 'trigger inferences' as Leroi Jones more compellingly re-christened them.[63] The prose moves rapidly and improvisationally, like jazz 'scatting', to describe the flitting 'bat subterraneans' (bat-like and/or 'batty') amongst which the morose and sententious Percepied haltingly lumbers, weighed down by his desire to take seriously his involvement with Mardou in a way she perhaps does not want. Arguably, the concept of 'love' is being opened up to a critique in this process—the way in which the term carries an underlay of 'possessiveness', with the partner being reduced to the status of a love-object—commodified by the ideological coding of 'love' in post-war white US culture. Leo's problems with negotiating any different cultural approach to love and sexuality open up a dialogue with other ways of understanding the term, hybridizing cultural expectations of what love constitutes and how some women want to see it. *The Subterraneans* explores this territory with a fierce intensity, generated by its rapid and excoriating spontaneous prose.

Having quickly produced in *The Subterraneans*, another experimental, intense and highly autobiographical work of fiction, Kerouac then turned back to revising *On the Road*—which he hoped was very close to publication (though things in fact worked out differently, since the novel only appeared in 1957, four years later). Much of this revision work was at the request of his Viking editors who felt some condensation of the cross-country trips was required. Kerouac was in a highly fraught state at this time, and during the course of possibly quite tense editorial meetings (during the fall of 1953), Viking's interest waned in spite of Cowley's continued support.

Despite this setback, Kerouac did, in response to Ginsberg's and Burroughs' enquiries, produce a concise account of his writing style, 'Essentials of Spontaneous Prose'. This short essay was a more thoughtful attempt than his slightly earlier 'Belief and Technique for Modern Prose', though it was not exactly an 'Essential' guide since it over-emphasized his particular interest at this time in Reich. Kerouac was also becoming involved with the New York Action painters, Pollock, Kline and de Kooning, and the stress his 'Essentials' places upon spontaneity, and its demand for absolutely no revision was to an extent influenced by their approach. Furthermore, he shared the Action painters' liking for prodigious amounts of alcohol; he was now drinking very heavily, using amphetamines and barbiturates frequently, and (relatedly) deteriorating physically. He was also fairly often at this time sleeping with men (such as Alan Ansen).

During 1953 Kerouac became increasingly interested in Buddhism, as was Allen Ginsberg. When Ginsberg set off for San Francisco via Mexico, Kerouac, encouraged by Neal Cassady, headed off to the West Coast as well, rejoining the

Cassadys in San Jose (at the time absorbed by prophet Edgar Cayce's theories of reincarnation and Oral Roberts' fundamentalist preaching). There Kerouac's interest in Buddhism (specifically Mahayana Buddhism) blossomed and he turned to Taoism. Zen was of less interest, though he liked and translated haiku, and wrote many of his own (the collection of his haiku published in 2003 contains many examples of this work). Falling out paranoidly with Cassady over how to divide up a consignment of marijuana leaves, he moved back into San Francisco, started writing *Some of the Dharma*, a huge compendium of meditations and writings about Buddhism, and commenced *San Francisco Blues*, the second of a series of *Books of Blues* 'choruses', drawing on 'jazz blues' structures.[64] (The first, 'Richmond Hill Blues', had been written some time in 1953). The bare structure of the choruses in these collections proved to be influential, as did their taking up of sense impressions (sights, sounds, smells) and reflections in the mind:

> I see the backs
> Of old Men rolling
> Slowly into black
> Stores
> ...
>   little girls make
>   shadows on the
>   sidewalk shorter
> than the shadow
>   of death
>   in this town—
>   (from 1st and 5th Choruses, *San Francisco Blues*)

Kerouac then returned to Richmond Hill (in April 1954) to continue his Buddhist studies and add sections to *Some of the Dharma*. He also wrote the bulk of a science fiction short story, 'cityCityCITY' (a Burroughsian allegory on McCarthyism). As ever, he was additionally rushing, often drunkenly, into and around New York, plagued by drink-induced phlebitis and pursued by Joan for maintenance. Yet still his work remained unpublished and, in his opinion, his literary agent was insufficiently active on his behalf.

Consequently, Malcolm Cowley's success in persuading *New World Writing* to feature Kerouac's 'Jazz of the Beat Generation', a patchwork of passages from *On the Road* and

Visions of Cody, was particularly significant. It perhaps encouraged Kerouac to turn back to further rewriting of *On the Road*, at the time entitled *The Beat Generation*. But drink and drug abuse and dependency increased, as did publishers' rejections, despite the efforts of Kerouac's new agent, Sterling Lord (who stayed loyal to him all his life).

Kerouac at this time contemplated starting a new work about his Lowell childhood, and moved back to Rocky Mount, using it as a base for New York visits. He was stuck in a cycle of poverty. However, writing continued rapidly: 'Bowery Blues', work on 'Wake Up' (or 'Buddha Tells Us', a handbook on Buddhism) and the completion of 'cityCityCITY'.

'cityCityCITY' is a dystopic science fiction vision of a future society controlled by 'Master Centre Love' ('MCL') and MCL's McCarthyite operatives such as G-92, who rule oppressively via a regime of surveillance over a city divided into 'blocks' kept rigidly separate from one another. The separation is sustained by the 'No-Zone' laws, which the city's controllers are resolved to enforce. These laws prohibit passage from all areas of cityCityCITY into the 'No-Zone' between them—the two being separated by an invisible and barely penetrable barrier. These constraints are designed to preserve social energy to ensure it remains centered on furthering 'Master Center Love' (191). Barrier-strengthening is required because occasional resistance emerges, manifested in the way that some of cityCityCITY's youths throw themselves against these barriers, usually bouncing off, but sometimes penetrating into the desired 'No-Zone' successfully. This is called 'Sexing' (191).

It is easy to read this vision of repressive policing of social behavior as a police-state allegory about the interface between political and sexual 'policing' in the McCarthy era, during which Communists and homosexuals were persecuted by the US State. In a sense, the repressive severity of the ideological constraints, rendered in the story as an invisible yet almost solid barrier, is a symptomatic indication of the instability of 'MCL'—that is, any attempt to sustain an inflexible version of sexuality constrained by domesticity and marriage as a heterosexual master-discourse. In other words, the very rigidity of the repressive apparatus (the cordoning off of the 'No-Zone') is in fact an indicator of underlying social tensions.

This Huxleyean and Burroughs-influenced satire on

McCarthyism is written in a densely packed, allusive prose which intimates that the outcome of this allegorical confrontation between the youths and 'MCL' hangs in the balance. It is a powerful, if difficult, piece of writing.

As 'cityCityCITY's completion alongside 'Bowery Blues' indicates, Kerouac was always at this time readily distracted by new projects, for example, returning to Lowell from New York to research a never-to-be-finished portrait of his place of birth, *A Book of Memory*, in late 1954. He also planned a novel entitled 'Visions of Bill'. But he was still shunned by publishers, and when 'Jazz of the Beat Generation' was published in April 1955 (under the name of Jean-Louis) in *New World Writing 7* it was his first publication in five years. It also marked the appearance of the new, post-*Town and the City* writing style that was to make him famous. His stock was rising.

The cover of *New World Writing* 7 (1955), headed up by Jack Kerouac's contribution, 'Jazz of the Beat Generation'.

Perhaps his high levels of productivity alongside this rare publication success caused Kerouac to become too egotistical and self-regarding at this point—a character trait that henceforth began to intensify and eventually alienate his friends as he shuttled between New York and North Carolina. Yet Cowley persisted in canvassing on his behalf. First he helped Kerouac get 'The Mexican Girl' section from *On the*

Road published in *Paris Review* (making eventual publication of the novel itself more probable; 'Mexican Girl' came out in *Paris Review* 11, 1955). Then he helped him get 'cityCityCITY' accepted by *The New American Reader* (though it was not to be published until 1959 when it appeared in the science fiction magazine *Nugget*). These successes stimulated Kerouac to write 'MacDougall Street Blues', yet another of his books of blues choruses. Meanwhile Cowley once again revived his interest in helping Kerouac get *On the Road* published.

Kerouac at this point revisited Mexico City, hoping the change would help cure his phlebitis. He stayed with Bill Garver, subsidized by a National Institute of Arts and Letters Award (again secured with Cowley's help). The freedom he felt in Mexico stimulated him to return to work: on his railroad novel, on ideas about writing *Visions of Gerard* and, in September 1955, on *Mexico City Blues*, a major 'set' in his sequence of blues 'choruses', each of which was to be rapidly completed in keeping with the spontaneous principles underlying all these blues poems' composition.

Mexico City Blues consists of 242 single-page improvisational poems, each of which stands as a more or less separate 'Chorus'. These choruses are shaped in terms of length and line-arrangement to fit into small pocket-sized notebooks. Improvised 'blues' choruses would be quickly scribbled down, sketching out Kerouac's observations, feelings and memories in an improvisational, loose jazz form consisting of fragmented visions. The poems blend Kerouac's interest in jazz, Buddhism and American culture with his memories of his Lowell past in a complex fusion. The '11th Chorus' is in many ways typical of the striking effects this apparently loose fusion can generate:

Brown wrote a book
The White and the Black

N a r c o t i c C i t y
switchin on

A n g e r F a l l s—

The Chorus then quite literally breaks off, until, at the bottom of the page, the words '(musician stops,/ brooding on the bandstand)' appear. In less than two dozen words, this

'Chorus' recreates the way a jazz musician tentatively launches out on a riff, then breaks off, pausing to search for inspiration, for a 'jewel centre' from which to take off. But, instantaneously, Kerouac takes us outside the jazz riff as the musician 'stops' playing to 'brood' upon the problem of achieving inspiration,and to consider how such brooding is tied to social and cultural coordinates. The musician's artistic crisis is juxtaposed with that of the writer, 'Brown', as he works on his book, experiencing the need to take on board the increasingly polarized divisions of racial discourse during the rise of Civil Rights (so 'Brown' *needs* to become 'Black' in the title of his own book). Kerouac's compressed poem makes plain how these tensions have social consequences ('Narcotic[s]' and 'Anger') and how injustice and inequality have stirred up rage and blighted America's belief in its special status as the world's first democracy ('Angel Falls' mutates into 'Anger Falls'—predicting the further rise of militant pride in blackness, as in the Black Power movement). Intertextually, Brown's 'book' is linked to Stendhal's *The Red and the Black* (set, pertinently, during the French Revolution—a revolution to secure *egalité*). Stendhal depicts a common man refusing to accede to any authority constraining his personal freedom, yet concealing this anarchic self under a veil of hypocrisy.[65] The writer (and also, metatextually, Kerouac himself, perplexed by issues of how to sustain authenticity) consequently has to break off to contemplate the knotty issues raised by entitling his story 'The White and the Black', when faced with a class-conscious and racist society. This sort of packed intensity characterizes many of what otherwise appear to be free-wheeling 'Blues' in Kerouac's many other *Books of Blues*, though recurrently any 'anger' his successive choruses contain is more than offset by a predominant sense of meditative Buddhist resignation ('One never dies/ One's never born'—'102nd Chorus').

In such blues poems, Kerouac concertedly embraced spontaneity. Most usually, the 'form' derived from the way jazz improvisation was determined by timing and by the musician's spontaneous 'phrasing & harmonizing' so that, as a result, 'It's all ... non stop ad libbing within each chorus' (*Book of Blues*, 1). This even extended to 'goofing'—a form of scat improvisation, as in '80th Chorus' from *Mexico City Blues*:

> GOOFING AT THE TABLE:
> "You just don't know."

"What don't I know?"
"How good this ham n eggs
    is
If you had any idea
    whatsoever
How good this is
Then you would stop
    writing poetry
And dig in." (*MCB*, 80)

Plainly a twofold mistrust of 'literature' exists: firstly, the poem suggests there is no way that words can fully convey the deliciousness of 'ham n eggs'; secondly, it proposes that writing is consequently a futile distraction—the poem actually undermines itself by suggesting its composition should 'stop'. And this self-undermining of poetry is written out in a language register that is distinctly not 'poeticised'. Yet, at the same time, paradoxically, the poem has a clear poetic debt—to William Carlos Williams' poem about stealing cold plums from the icebox, entitled 'This Is Just To Say'. Williams' poem takes up what might be the exact wording used on a scribbled note left on an icebox door and arranges it into line-patterns and stanzaic arrangements, thereby visually signaling that these words now stand in a poem: 'This is just to say/ I have eaten the plums/ that were in the icebox/ and which you were/ probably/ saving for breakfast'.[66] Williams' poem stands as a clear forebear of Kerouac's '80th Chorus'.[67] Just like Kerouac's 'Chorus', 'This Is Just To Say' interrogates its own status, as its title indicates, by calling into question the significance of both the particular poem itself and 'the poem' in general. In the same way, Kerouac's '80th Chorus' appears to be simply a straightforward transcription of a conversation between two individuals, one of them happening to be a poet. Yet, quite plainly, Kerouac's poem is also raising the issue of what constitutes the divide between art and (what might be called) 'non-art': be this ordinary conversation or simply eating 'ham n eggs'. Kerouac is making the implicit point that he, like Williams, wants to extend the boundaries of what might be considered to be art. The implicit question is, on whose *author*ity are the boundaries between art and 'non-art' drawn up? Just as Williams once wrote a poem centering on an old man employed to clear away 'dog lime', Kerouac climaxes one of his 'Choruses' by describing 'Lantern jawed junkmen' on '3rd St Market' who 'Came, bending to spit,/ &

Shuffled awhile there' ('San Francisco Blues', *Book of Blues*, 7). Kerouac's aim is always to observe his own injunction in 'Essentials of Spontaneous Prose': 'never defray impressions'.[68]

As Robert Creeley notes in his introduction to *Book of Blues* in 1995 (which collects Kerouac's many *Books of Blues* together), Kerouac's long series of rapidly-improvised blues sequences became influential. Circulated informally, often in manuscript form, amongst the poets loosely associated with the Beats (only *Mexico City Blues* was to be published near-contemporaneously), they caused a stir owing to the way they redefined how poetry writing might be understood.

At this time in Mexico, Kerouac was also conducting a strange, obsessive and perhaps one-way love affair with a Mexico City prostitute, Esperanza Tercero (***Tristessa***), and writing up a story about this in August ('Trembling and Chaste', the first half of *Tristessa*). Kerouac, on completing the story and quite unable to bring himself to commit to Tercero, left Mexico City in September 1955 and, with the help of a lift from a blonde-haired female—an event written up as the story 'Good Blonde' years later—returned to San Francisco (as retold in ***Dharma Bums***).

In San Francisco Kerouac met a new circle of Ginsberg's friends, including Philip Whalen, Michael McClure, Lawrence Ferlinghetti, Kenneth Rexroth, and Gary Snyder. He quickly became especially friendly with Snyder, though Snyder's Zen Buddhism and Kerouac's rather idiosyncratic Mahayana Buddhism meshed poorly. Kerouac also attended the famous '6 Poets at 6 Gallery' reading on 13 October 1955,[69] which was intended to mark the public emergence of the 'San Francisco Renaissance'. This 6 Gallery linking-up of the 'Berkeley Renaissance' poets with other San Franciscan poets was, however, somewhat upstaged by the New York Beat 'carpetbaggers', particularly when Ginsberg performed his first full public reading of 'HOWL' (Kerouac was too shy to perform). As Michael McClure put it, 'a barrier had been broken'.[70] Whilst it is an exaggeration to say this event founded the San Francisco Renaissance it was important in promoting the various post-war San Francisco poetry movements and in helping cement links with other writers, shaping what became the 'New American Poetry': the New York poets, the Black Mountain poets and the Deep Image poets, as well as the Beats.[71]

Kerouac went on to stay with Snyder in his cottage and took part in various group-sex activities (as retold in ***The Dharma Bums***), though his participation was limited, constrained, and accompanied by an open misogyny. He was still drinking excessively and, in addition, becoming overtly homophobic. Snyder also detected at this time a 'palpable aura of fame and death' around Kerouac.[72] This was a sign that, though even *On the Road* still remained unpublished, Kerouac was attracting celebrity to himself via his various writing exploits, his personal lifestyle, and legends about both.

Negotiations to get *On the Road* published still continued (it was back with Viking Press), but so did Kerouac's drinking binges. Snyder took him mountain hiking (on one occasion with a librarian, John Montgomery) partly to get him away from such bingeing. On these hikes, Snyder also tutored Kerouac in the ways of environmentalism.

However, returning to the Coast, Kerouac, with increasing frequency, escalated his anti-social behavior whenever he was drunk—and he frequently was. He had also become very anti-Communist. He revisited the Cassady home and there attended an unorthodox Church service and met a liberal Catholic bishop (the basis of the play, ***The Beat Generation*** and the film, ***Pull My Daisy***). Neal and Carolyn had effectively separated but when Neal's new woman, Natalie Johnson, committed suicide (as retold in ***Dharma Bums***), Neal returned home. So, when Kerouac fell out with almost everyone in San Francisco, and very badly with Allen Ginsberg, he left to join Neal and Carolyn in Los Gatos.

In Los Gatos Kerouac soon wanted out, unable to cope with the tense triangle that re-emerged between him, Neal and Carolyn, and resolved, with Snyder's encouragement, to become a fire lookout (as retold in ***Dharma Bums***). First, however, he launched out on another trans-American journey. He revisited Rocky Mount and there wrote *Visions of Gerard* in December and January 1955-56, again using benzedrine to sustain his effort. The work probably incorporated earlier writings about 'Gerard', a fictionalized version of Kerouac's brother, Francis Gerard Kéroack.

Visions of Gerard is a representation of the illness and death of a young boy, Gerard, in 1920s' Lowell, viewed through the eyes of his younger brother, Ti-Jean. Ti-Jean narrates his memories as an adult, looking back from the 1950s. Ti Jean emphasizes the saintliness of Gerard and how this is made manifest in a vision Gerard has at school of his ascension to heaven just before the terminal stage of his illness. Gerard also has a rapport with animals and birds, berating his cat over the killing of a mouse and attracting a flock of birds to his bedroom window as a bed-ridden invalid. This reputation for beatitude leads the nuns who taught him at school to be present at his death-bed and record his final words. His saintliness is underlined when, immediately after his death, 'the flock of birds ... phebes and peewits ... that had pestered at his window for so long since Spring broke in, was gone' (137).

Visions of Gerard has little plot, instead simply describing the decline, death and funeral of Gerard. The book does, however, possess a central theme, which, roughly speaking, is that life is just an illusion and, therefore, '"Don't you realize you are God?"' (138). This is a symptom of Kerouac's growing Buddhism ('That ... there *seems* to be a world, is hugely more interesting than what ... might happen in it'—122-3). This leitmotif of the book links up with its exploration of pre-war Catholic Lowell through the saintly, but distinctly Buddhistic reflections of Gerard, who urges his brother to spare all animals and insects and follow his own example: '"The little flies too, you dont have to kill them—they rub their little legs"' (125).

Gerard's life consequently proves to be an inspiration for Ti-Jean, the source of his orientation towards the spiritual and, ultimately, towards depicting this spiritual world verbally. But Gerard's illness and death have another effect on Ti-Jean, which emerges through *Visions of Gerard*'s stress both on the poverty and unemployment commonly found in working class Lowell in the 1920s and on how these often lead to deprivation and illness.[73] At one point, Gerard brings home a starving boy he found in Lowell, and all of Gerard's family suffer from complaints—'his aunt, all his uncles all invalids—all in pain—Suffering and pain' (70).

This context casts a bitter light on their father's contention that 'in life it's a jungle, man eats man either you eat or get eaten ... It's like that, life' (20). Emil Duluoz is here answering a query put to him by Gerard: 'Why we were made to suffer and be harsh in return' (13). It also helps explain the appearance of 'muckchop rich ... Mr. Groscorp' at the end of the novella, devouring a large meal whilst watching, through a window, the passing funeral cortege of Gerard. The often sharp division in the 1920s between wealth and poverty is thus highlighted at the very moment in the text when Gerard's wasted body is being buried.

In a sense, there is a sort of internal debate going on in this text between, on the one hand, the book's Buddhistic insistence on acceptance and, on the other, its frank portrait of deprivation and poverty, with (perhaps) the balance tilting towards advocating a muted kind of personal political involvement. After all, it should be noted that Gerard in fact intervenes—seeking to save not only animals, birds and insects but also to feed a hungry child he meets. Perhaps this subdued political conscience is prompted by the 1950s' perspective brought to the events. Ti-Jean, looking back, has an awareness of the way that, though 1950s' affluence is not universal, the decade's preponderant well-being creates a large corps of comfortably off, suburban whites, happy to insulate themselves from the existence of continued suffering, like the pre-war Mr. Groscorp. *Visions of Gerard* is most certainly a warm portrait by Ti Jean of memories of his older brother, but it is also, more than this, a novel wrestling with the issue of expressing effective social concern.

Perhaps Kerouac's use of benzedrine when writing *Visions of Gerard* was necessary to support him through the painful process of recalling his brother's life. To recover from the effort, Kerouac spent a brief period in New York, once again drinking excessively, but also writing 'Brooklyn Bridge Blues'. Returning to his sister in North Carolina, he worked on *Tristessa* some more, as well as 'Visions of Lucien', and an evolving *Book of Dreams*. He also put further work into the Buddhistic *Some of the Dharma* (completing this in March 1956), and commenced a 'Book of Prayer'. He became very friendly with his young nephew, but began to fall out with his brother-in-law (as retold in ***Dharma Bums***).

Accordingly, he decamped to Snyder's cabin on the West Coast, writing at Snyder's instigation *The Scripture of the Golden Eternity*, an attempt at a Buddhist sutra, but one somewhat compromised by his residual Catholic belief in God. He then (in May 1956) commenced a piece of experimental writing called, alternatively, 'Sebastian' or 'Lucien Midnight'. This was to evolve gradually into the highly experimental, Joyce-influenced *Old Angel Midnight*. Snyder provided Kerouac with a calm environment, further hiking and more tuition in the arts of living with nature (as narrated in ***The Dharma Bums***). Snyder also, with Ginsberg in support, introduced

Kerouac to more West Coast luminaries: principally Alan Watts, an authority on Buddhism, and the poets Ed Dorn and Robert Creeley. Creeley was keen to meet Kerouac after reading 'The Mexican Girl' in *The Paris Review*--his admiration later leading him to publish the first part of 'The Railroad Earth' and 'Essentials of Spontaneous Prose' in the little literary magazine he edited, *Black Mountain Review*. Kerouac also cemented other West Coast friendships (with Lamantia—an old friend, and with Michael McClure, who published a chorus from *Mexico City Blues* in the literary review *Ark II Moby I* in 1956/57).

Snyder departed to study in Japan, after recognizing how far gone Kerouac was because of his alcoholism. Kerouac now participated in what had become a habitual, hectic, drunken merry-go-round, taking in Cassady, Bob Kaufman, a reluctant Kenneth Rexroth and, especially, Creeley, who became his regular drinking companion. However, Kerouac's recent hikes with Snyder and a new cure for phlebitis (achieved by standing on his head) had made him healthier than he had been for a while. So in June 1956 he was able to report to a fire-watching training camp, before commencing fire-watching duties on Desolation Peak in the Cascades (***Dharma Bums***; **'Alone on a Mountain Top'** in ***Lonesome Traveler***; ***Desolation Angels***). He was to keep returning to this fire-watching episode in his fiction, perhaps indicating the seminal significance of this moment in his life which he called a 'turningabout' (*DA*, 305) and which was certainly a turning point. The spell on Desolation Peak was not a success in terms of his writing output, however: he kept a journal, but produced little else.

The Mademoiselle image, as it appeared in the *New York Times* in 1957, with the crucifix cropped out. Kerouac was often to complain about this editing, which frequently occurred.

After the fire-watch ended, Kerouac traveled down, via Seattle, to San Francisco, where the San Francisco Renaissance was in full, exciting flood. There he began unavoidably to negotiate his increasing fame generated by a trickle of publications, Ginsberg's publicity efforts and Viking's decision to accept *On the Road* (as retold in ***Desolation Angels***). His growing reputation even led to a photographic session for the cover of *Mademoiselle* in September 1956. The famous image that resulted depicted him wearing an open-neck check shirt (he had just completed his fire-watching) and wearing a crucifix (Kerouac complained that many of the press outlets using this photograph doctored it to remove the crucifix).

At this time, perhaps fired up by this growing attention, Kerouac also started a new round of dissolute excess; even a growing friendship with Peter Orlovsky could not slow his corrosive decline. His Buddhism lapsed. He spent some time at Los Gatos with the Cassadys, where Carolyn found him 'lost and morose', and then set off via Los Angeles for Mexico City (***Desolation Angels***).

In Mexico City he rejoined Bill Garver (***Tristessa***), re-encountered Esperanza briefly, was rolled by some Mexican hoodlums and completed *Tristessa* in the Autumn of 1956.

Tristessa depicts two visits made to Mexico City in 1955 and 1956 by the novel's narrator, Jack Duluoz. He stays with a friend, Bull Gaines (an addict), and becomes involved with Tristessa (a prostitute and Bull's morphine supplier). Duluoz becomes sexually attracted to Tristessa and the book explores the way that Duluoz finds it difficult to confront the ramifications of this desire. Instead, a frustrated Duluoz, half-heartedly sworn to celibacy because of his Buddhist beliefs, hangs around his two addict-acquaintances, watching them score, shoot-up, and lie around as their condition declines. Finally he leaves, but Tristessa plays on his mind. He returns to Mexico City, only to find Tristessa has deteriorated markedly.

Duluoz travels to Mexico City as a practicing Buddhist sworn to chastity, and this complicates his growing infatuation with Tristessa. The novel records the resulting dilemmas, so the text can be read as the story of a 'doomed' love affair between the two. In part, this is plainly what it is, but it is also an exploration of how Duluoz is forced to remain the perpetual outsider. He is locked outside Mexican life as a tourist and locked outside the junky lifestyles of Tristessa and Bull, both because of his own failings—chiefly his failure to understand Tristessa's motivations and needs—and because of Bull's and Tristessa's morphine-dominated preoccupations. Despite his compassion for these two Mexico City addicts' sickness, Jack is trapped in an anguished struggle with his desires from which he cannot break free. The failure of the nascent affair is a symptom of Jack's inevitable exclusion from Tristessa's drug-taking circle, rather than a love story to be isolated in its own right, despite his wish to do this. He and Tristessa are hopelessly mismatched, but his sentimental romanticization of Tristessa's 'native' allure draw him into an emotional engagement harmful to them both.

This story is told in the present tense, economically conveying Jack's inability to distance himself from his narrative. Initially it is presented as a confusing melange of dream and wakefulness. Though the resulting narrative is laced with stereotyping of Mexico and its capital city, it also projects an awareness of Jack's 'white American tourist' reflexes, as when Jack tips a cab-driver and worries whether, 'Tristessa thinks I am too splurgey like big John Drunk in Mexico' (9). Jack senses he is an excluded outsider, and this exacerbates the misapprehensions that underlie his infatuation with Tristessa. She should—indeed must necessarily—remain 'the girl of his *dreams*': Jack's descriptions of Tristessa are laced with a disturbing melancholic eroticism that both idealizes her and undercuts his Buddhistic commitment to celibacy.

On his second trip, when he discovers a severely deteriorated Tristessa, Jack recognizes the gulf is unbridgeable. This gulf, he also understands, does not stem solely from his half-convinced vow of chastity. What really held him back from propositioning Tristessa was fear of rejection, based on an unconscious recognition that her status as a junky disqualifies her from committing to enduring attachments. Tristessa has been a junky since sixteen and her life revolves around the need to satisfy her addiction. So Jack perpetually fails to achieve communication; they have different 'mental radios' (42). Bull, unlike Jack, can communicate with Tristessa, using 'routine junkey talk in baby Spanish' (94). Jack recognizes that this sort of intimacy lies beyond him, not least because 'morphine takes all the sex out of your parts and leaves it somewhere else' (95). Or as Tristessa puts it, '"I no awanta love"'. Jack's fictionalized memoir adeptly questions the apparent self-explanatoriness of the term 'love', which his sentimental narrative had at first unthinkingly embraced. Instead the text implicitly focuses upon how love is allocated different semantic weightings within different cultures, and how Jack's half-hearted 'love' for

Tristessa may actually have deeply disturbed her and contributed to her decline. Like *Maggie Cassidy* and *The Subterraneans*, then, *Tristessa* is in large part a reflection upon love that upsets assumptions that 'love' is somehow a natural 'given', rather than culturally constructed. It is another powerful text exposing the tangle of motivations the term conceals. Like *The Subterraneans*, too, the novella is excoriatingly autobiographical.

Having despaired of his Buddhist vows and with Esperanza Tercero lost to drug addiction, Kerouac turned again to Mexican prostitutes. When Ginsberg, Corso, and Peter and Lafcadio Orlovsky joined him in late 1956, they also sometimes engaged (male) prostitutes, and the resulting caravansary traveled around Mexico (as retold in ***Desolation Angels***). At this time *The Subterraneans* was accepted for publication by Grove Press's *Evergreen Review* (though what Kerouac saw as Donald Allen's intrusive editing derailed this and the work was not to be released—as a stand-alone novel—until 1959). Kerouac's fame as well as that of all the 'Beats' was waxing. Corso went to Washington to do some Library of Congress readings for Randall Jarrell, whilst the others returned to New York City. In New York, Kerouac met and developed a relationship with Helen Weaver (see ***Desolation Angels***). He was also writing hard: finishing off *Tristessa* and working both on *Desolation Angels* and on pre-publication revisions of *On the Road*, in consultation with Malcolm Cowley. Four years of revisions had by now built up. Kerouac consequently chose to type up a new version, returning to the original scroll and the 1952 retyping for fresh inspiration. Comparison of the scroll with the final published version shows that Kerouac was by 1956-57 prepared to countenance some significant changes. For example, consider the following two passages, one taken from the scroll and the other from the published book:

> 1951 *Scroll*: ... he had to sweat and curse to make a living and so on. My first impression of Neal was of a young Gene Autry—trim, thin-hipped, blue eyes, with a real Oklahoma accent. In fact he'd just been working on a ranch.
>
> 1957 *Book*: ... he had to sweat and curse to make a living and so on. You saw that in the way he stood bobbing his head, always looking down, nodding, like a young boxer to instructions, throwing in a thousand 'Yeses' and 'That's rights'. My first impression of Dean was of a young Gene Autry—trim, thin-

> hipped, blue-eyed, with a real Oklahoma accent—a side-burned hero of the snowy West. In fact he'd just been working on a ranch. (*OR*, 6)

A slightly greater instability in Dean can be detected in the 1957 version. He is now more plainly represented as a site of conflict in Sal's portrait: like a young boxer on the one hand—slightly excessive in his desire to please and slightly too fired-up—whilst on the other mythologized, less reliably, as 'a side-burned hero of the snowy West' in line with Sal's tendency to romanticize. Such changes make it clear why Cowley once claimed that Kerouac was 'good [at] revision' (Gifford and Lee, *Jack's Book*, p.206). However, there were some losses: pseudonyms were introduced (the scroll used the real names of the protagonists (Ginsberg, Cassady, Burroughs, etc.) and the novel lost some of the raw energy of the scroll. It became an ever more edited, ever more mediated work: for example, extracts from Cassady's diaries were introduced,[74] whilst some self-censorship occurred, particularly of the more explicit homosexual scenes. In December 1956 this more 'literary' *On the Road* was at last accepted by Viking.

Meanwhile, drink and drugs had badly eroded Kerouac's relationship with Helen Weaver, so he deserted her to travel to Florida for Christmas where his sister had moved with Mémêre. He traveled there by way of Washington, where Gregory Corso was still staying with the Jarrells, in December 1956. In Washington he stopped over for a while to write 'Washington D.C. Blues' (as retold in ***Desolation Angels***).

On arriving in Florida Kerouac worked on the writing done in Mexico and then returned to New York. But there he found it difficult to bear what he called 'the hectic "fame" life'.[75] He escaped NYC to travel with Ginsberg to Rutherford to meet William Carlos Williams in January 1957, but another chaotic round of New York socializing immediately followed (see ***Desolation Angels***). Helen broke off with him and he established a new relationship, with Joyce Glassman.

Almost immediately, once again unable to sustain a relationship with a woman, Kerouac left America for Tangiers to visit Burroughs (**'Big Trip to Europe'**, in ***Lonesome Traveler***; ***Desolation Angels***). There he read Genet, helped Burroughs with his *Naked Lunch* manuscript by typing out large amounts of it at his usual lightning speed, and indulged in Moroccan prostitutes (see ***Desolation Angels***). He also began to plan the writing of *The Dharma Bums*. He was, however, very unhappy when he saw Donald Allen's editing of *The Subterraneans* for *Evergreen Review* and decided to withdraw it. He was equally upset by Viking's rejection of both *Doctor Sax* and a version of the first part of *Desolation Angels*. Ginsberg and Orlovsky at this point arrived in Tangiers, but, distressed and homesick, Kerouac shortly after their arrival set off for Marseilles, Paris (where he met up with Corso), and London before returning to America (as retold in ***Desolation Angels***). There he carried out a plan to move Mémêre to Berkeley from Florida.

Things became briefly more settled: Joan wanted to divorce him to remarry; Kerouac started writing again—carrying out more work on *The Book of Dreams*, 'Lucien Midnight' and later sections of *Desolation Angels*; and Donald Allen agreed to replace *The Subterraneans* with the second part of 'The Railroad Earth' in the Summer 1957 issue of *Evergreen Review*.

The cover design of *Evergreen Review* Vol. 1 No. 2, the famous 'San Francisco Scene' issue, which carried Kerouac's 'October in the Railroad Earth'.

'The Railroad Earth'[76] is a long, often flowing, memoir recounting the narrator's memories of his experiences as a 'student brakeman' on the Southern Pacific Railroad in California. Its structure is episodic: its fifteen sections are loosely linked together by being set in the month of 'October' (it was originally called 'October in the Railroad Earth'), and by focusing on the narrator's early career on the railroad.

The sections shunt backwards and forwards through Jack's memory, arranged around the hub of two October Sundays spent at work. Sections 4, 5 and 6 deal with one of these Sundays and sections 12, 13 and 14 with the other—the two days linked by the fact that on the first Sunday Jack narrowly misses the train to which he has been assigned as brakeman, whilst on the second he just manages to catch it. Interspersed are other memories: of other days; of the streets of San Francisco linking the rail yards and the flophouse where he sleeps; of the experience of working in the yards; of the sights to be seen traveling along the railroad; and finally, his memories of the 'first run I ever made' on the railroad (57). That the story ends with a memory of his very first day at work underlines how the narrative constantly shifts from the narrative present backwards, to memories of the two central Sundays and, beyond these, to other days during his spell as a student brakeman. A complex tapestry of impressions and memories results, conveyed at times in some of the best writing to be found in Kerouac's oeuvre. At times the narrative becomes slightly sentimental, underlining the romanticized role assigned to the railroad in American history, but the main emphasis falls upon portraying demanding railroad work and the scenes of poverty and deprivation alongside the tracks witnessed by this ordinary working man.

The narrative highlights the mixed experiences of manual labor: the way in which pleasure can be taken in the manual dexterity and athletic prowess brought to the job, but also the way that unremitting pressure introduces real dangers into the work—the constant risk of accidents. As a fellow railroad worker observes, '"That's the trouble with the railroad, you always gotta get there fast"' (45). The fiction of the nobility of work is comprehensively undercut, and labor's actual precariousness, with its risk of instant job-dismissal, exists as a constant chorus. This is set against the background of the 'well-dressed' Bay Area commuters and 'the impending rush of their commuter frenzy' (119) passing the 'bums' of Third Street by the railroad yards. These intersections lay down the class lines of America that frame the 'romance' of the railroad, so steadily deconstructing it. The railroad instead is portrayed as a point of intersection of social and class relations in America's 'Steel civilization' (119).

In all this, Jack remains unfixed from any sure social location—uneasily neither inside nor outside the railroad workers' culture. The narrative shuttle between past and present tense helps emphasize his unstable and shifting relationship to this world of work. Jack largely remains an alienated outsider, and this becomes a powerful metaphor for the position of a significant number of young people touched by World War Two, and uneasy with their positions in a post-war America within which they can find no certain place. This story offers a powerful portrait of their ambiguous station in life.

Helped by this publication of the first part of 'The Railroad Earth' in the widely noticed 'San Francisco Scene' issue of *Evergreen Review* in 1957, and slightly earlier by the appearance of the 'Cody and the Three Stooges' section from *Visions of Cody* in *New Directions*, Kerouac's reputation was rapidly growing. But so too, once more, was his binge drinking, and an increasingly close and in many ways destructive relationship with his mother.

In combination, their effect was deleterious; Kerouac could not handle his growing reputation or his drinking problem. He was also becoming increasingly self-opinionated and conceited. Finally, pressurized by his mother, he left San Francisco and returned to Orlando (in mid 1957), but not before advance copies of *On the Road* arrived in Berkeley, almost at the same time as Cassady, LuAnne and Hinkle happened to visit him (see ***Desolation Angels***).

As Kerouac read through the published version of *On the Road*, he perhaps recognized how significantly different this book was from the scroll version composed in 1951 and his experimental reworkings of 1951-52 that mostly ended up in *Visions of Cody*. The scroll, for example, was far more explicit about the Beats' homosexualities:

> **1951 Scroll**: Allen was queer in those days, experimenting with himself to the hilt, and Neal saw this ... [as] a former boyhood hustler in the Denver night ... I was in the same room. I heard them across the darkness and I mused and said to myself "Hmm, now something's started and I don't want anything to do with it."
>
> **1957 *Road***: Their energies met head-on, I was a lout compared, I couldn't keep up with them ... Wanting dearly to learn to write like Carlo, the first thing you know, Dean was attacking him with a great amorous souls such as only a con-man can have ... I didn't see them for about two weeks, during which time they cemented their relationship to fiendish allday-allnight-talk proportions. (8)

Certainly one of the unanswerable questions of post-war American literature must be: what sort of impact would the publication of the scroll version of *On the Road* have had if it had been published, as it could have been, in 1952? Perhaps Kerouac pondered this question in Orlando as he scanned the published work.

After a short period in Florida, where he installed Mémêre close to his sister Nin's house, he again returned to Mexico

City but only briefly (his departure precipitated by Bill Garver's suicide and an earthquake), before returning to Orlando and Mémêre. He worked at this time on his novellas about Burroughs (now called 'Secret Mullings about Bill') and Gary Snyder ('Visions of Gary').

The cover design of the first edition of *On the Road* (1957).

At this point another major transforming moment occurred. *On the Road* reached the bookshops on 5 September 1957. It received mixed reviews, though on balance hostile ones came to predominate—at least in the popular press. (Gilbert Millstein, in *The New York Times*, one of the first to review it, gave his enthusiastic support.) But this was almost unimportant: Kerouac was swept up by the publicity and the advance reputation of *On the Road* which had granted the novel a certain cult mystique, especially because of its association with the Beat phenomenon which had ignited after the publication of Ginsberg's *HOWL* in 1956 and all the ensuing censorship controversy. As Kerouac put it, 'everything exploded',[77] and his drunkenness and egotistical self-aggrandizing reached new heights as a consequence. He commenced negotiating film rights and it rained 'girls girls girls'.[78] *On the Road* also sold quite well and Grove resolved to bring out an unabridged, hard-cover edition of *The Subterraneans*. His career had taken off, but the benefits proved nugatory and the downsides disastrous.

Chapter Five: From *The Dharma Bums* to *Big Sur*

Even though he had moved on as a writer—indeed by January 1958 he was even claiming to dislike *On the Road*—Kerouac could cash in on his sudden fame. Soon after *On the Road*'s release in 1957 he drafted a play, 'The Beat Generation', which failed to reach the stage (though the script was re-discovered and published in 2005). This drew heavily on his memories of recent conversations with the Cassadys and their circle in California at that time, including a trip to a horseracing track and the visit of a progressive Roman Catholic bishop to their house (see Act 3 of the play). He also started work on a novel of childhood, 'Memory Babe', and wrote a preface for a book of photographs, *The Americans*, by a new friend, Robert Frank. Additionally, he became concerned to try to define 'the beat generation', emphasizing the beatific aspect of beatness in a series of articles, including 'The Philosophy of the Beat Generation' for *Esquire*.

This interest was in part provoked by ever-rising media attention, climaxing in a *Playboy* photo-shoot and some TV appearances, during one of which, famously, Truman Capote accused Kerouac of 'just typing' and 'not writing'.[79] This was part of a larger backlash against Kerouac, climaxing in Norman Podhoretz's attack in *Partisan Review* in the Spring of 1958, entitled 'The Know-Nothing Bohemians'. But the novel nevertheless immediately became a bestseller. Many women sought him out to sleep with him. Partly as a result he and Joyce split up, and despite attempts to renew relationships (with Helen Weaver, Edie Parker and Gary Snyder's ex-wife) a long period without any stable relationship ensued. His inability to handle fame rapidly took over: the demands of celebrity simply proved all but incompatible with his constant, paradox-ridden quest for authenticity. Ironically, despite his success and fame, Viking took a look at his pile of other manuscripts and turned them all down, to his immediate despair.

His drinking had by now made him almost impotent. However, his lionization meant that more of his work was getting accepted or being solicited. Back in Florida, he wrote *Orlando Blues*, another in his sequence of *Blues* choruses, to meet this demand, and also revived his attempt to write a Proustian evocation of Lowell, 'Memory Babe'. Paul Carroll accepted part of 'Lucien Midnight' for *Big Table* and James Laughlin agreed to publish excerpts from *Visions of Cody*, in a limited edition of 750 copies. Kerouac signed the final page of every single copy of these excerpts when the book was printed which suggests that though he later expressed reservations about the abridgement he was prepared to endorse it at the time.

Excerpts from Visions of Cody was to be a lot shorter than the full version, not published until 1972 and deemed to be 'unpublishable' in 1959 (as stated in a publicity flier for *Excerpts from Visions of Cody* inserted into the book). Most of the omitted material consists of the majority of *Visions of Cody*'s opening sketches, almost all of the tape transcriptions and much of the 'Imitation of the Tape' section. What results is a much more user-friendly text and, arguably, *Excerpts* still contains most of the best writing found in the later, uncut version. Its neglect seems unreasonable, especially since those who read it at the time obtained a sight of some of the best experimental writing Kerouac produced between 1951 and 1953 to set alongside some of the weaker writing that followed *On the Road*'s publication, when his addictions and celebrity status undermined him.

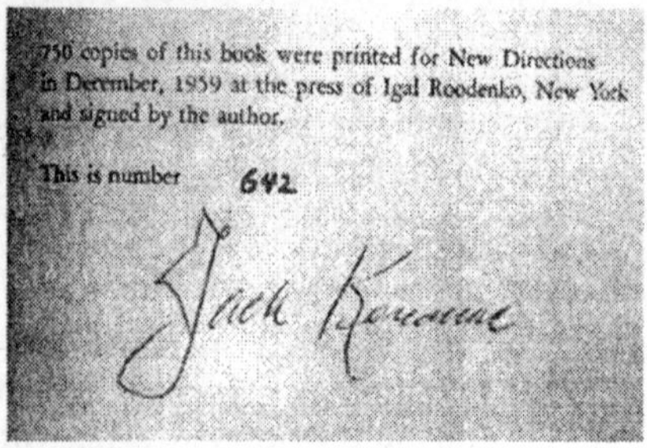
750 copies of this book were printed for New Directions in December, 1959 at the press of Igal Roodenko, New York and signed by the author.

This is number 642

The signature of Jack Kerouac on the final page of *Excerpts from Visions of Cody*, 1959.

Otherwise, his biggest achievement in late 1957 was to write *The Dharma Bums*, in ten sessions during November 1957 in spite of his severe alcoholism, as a quick follow-up to *On the Road*—a sequel, as it were, delivered at Viking's request.

The Dharma Bums is its narrator Ray Smith's account of his Buddhistic endeavors to understand the way of the Dharma (spiritual, blissful truth). The narrative details his encounter with Japhy Ryder, an exponent of another type of Buddhism, more oriented towards Zen than Smith's Mahayana Buddhism.[80] The distinction between the two is not really clarified in the book, but Smith seeks to be more constantly contemplative and ascetic than Ryder,[81] though unsure if he wants this asceticism to include celibacy. At the start of his narrative he explains how he has refrained from sex for some time, but early on he abandons this resolve, indulging in yabyum (a session of erotic sex) with Ryder, Alvah Goldbrook and a woman called 'Princess'. After this lapse, however, he rarely seeks out sexual partners. Ryder, by contrast, voraciously enjoys sexual encounters.

However, their common-yet-differing grasps of Buddhism are also informed by their American identities.[82] Ryder's enjoyment of nature is in part shaped by the way Buddhists recurrently seek solitary contemplation. This is the strand of Buddhism to which Smith is attracted as a result of meeting Ryder. But Ryder's return to nature is also part of the American western myth of wilderness as expounded by environmentalist John Muir and others, and much of the narrative describes how Ryder teaches Smith to travel in the 'wild'. To this extent the novel can serve as an environmental 'how to' manual, describing their hikes in the West Coast mountains. Eventually, Ryder persuades Smith to follow his example and become a fire lookout and the book's ending sees Smith fire-watching in the Cascades.

Both men are also poets, involved in the San Francisco poetry scene. An early incident in the book is a poetry reading: Ryder is a participant, Smith an involved spectator. This is described as 'the birth of the San Francisco Poetry Renaissance' (13). In historical fact it was the famous 1955 '6 Poets at 6 Gallery' reading,[83] at which Allen Ginsberg first read his poem 'HOWL' in public (in *The Dharma Bums*, 'Alvah Goldbrook' reads out 'Wail'—*DB*,14).

Other aspects of the cultural atmosphere and history of mid-fifties' San Francisco bohemia also emerge. Ryder's philosophy of independent communalism plainly relates to the species of anarchism fostered on the West Coast by its tradition of non-conformity and the influence of World War Two's West Coast Conscientious Objector camps. His philosophy also possesses continuities with a tradition of anarchistic and socialist thinking in the USA, particularly with the International Workers of the World (or Wobblies), the 'old I.W.W. mythology' (9). It is not just a generalized wilderness movement with which Ryder engages, but also a political matrix with specific West Coast inflections. Ryder describes this as providing the basis for a 'great rucksack revolution': 'thousands or even millions of young Americans wandering around' (97).

Smith finds all of this a heady brew. Though at times he draws back from adulation and criticizes selfish traits in himself and Ryder, the book is more firmly didactic than Kerouac's previous writings. There is little sense of class and class relations, though Ryder's working-class background helps him slough off 1950s' materialism. Smith does follow in Ryder's footsteps but, as Ryder goes off to Japan, he ends his stay on the Cascades without having resolved anything, *The Dharma Bums* symptomatically ends in anti-climax.

Kerouac's self-indulgent excesses and depressions meant that things could not flow his way for long. When he put together his *Book of Blues* (incorporating everything from *San Francisco Blues* to *Orlando Blues*) it was rejected by Ferlinghetti (as 'not poetry').[84] After some early success performing jazz-poetry readings with David Amram, a young musician, Kerouac's attempt to read his poems in a regular night club spot at New York's Vanguard during Christmas 1957 often flopped disastrously, though some of these jazz readings (often accompanied by Steve Allen) worked better than others, and Kerouac continued such experiments intermittently later on (again often with Steve Allen). He was by now so often drunk (and sometimes drugged too) that he was alienating almost everybody.

In January 1958 he returned to Florida and retyped *The Dharma Bums*, but *The Subterraneans* had come out to execrable reviews and his deterioration continued. Despite these reviews, however, his books were selling and back in New York, Grove agreed to bring out *Doctor Sax*. In order to move his mother up to New York (to Gilbert Street, Northport), he traveled back down to Florida with Robert Frank. With Frank, on the journey, he created a piece of collaborative photo-journalism, 'On the Road to Florida'. Intended for *Life*, this finally appeared in *Evergreen Review* (in 1970, long after his death). However, in Florida he became even more reclusive and paranoid, encouraged by Mémêre, with whom his relationship was becoming increasingly oedipal, as she took greater control of his affairs. Poor reviews of first, *The Subterraneans* in March, and then *The Dharma Bums* in the Fall, augmented his decline into despair during 1958. This melded poorly with his residual exhilaration over his media lionization and the recognition it carried. The mixed messages were leading, effectively, to a breakdown precipitated by his drinking problems. Yet he also continued to work through this period and participated in a debate at Brandeis where he read out his essay 'The Origins of the Beat Generation' (later revised and published in *Playboy* in 1959). More usually, however, he caroused in New York where a reconciliation with Joyce Glassman ended when in October 1958 he struck up a relationship with Dodie James Müller.

The Winter of 1958-9 was spent primarily attending to the demands that his success placed upon his workload whilst struggling with his alcoholism. He did, however, carry out some improvisational work on what would become the film *Pull My Daisy* (1959) with Robert Frank and Alfred Leslie—the script drawing on Act 3 of his play, *The Beat Generation*, and largely based on Kerouac's 1955 meeting with a progressive bishop in Cassady's home. He also worked on the essays 'New York Scenes' and 'The Vanishing American Hobo' with the help of Allen Ginsberg, Peter Orlovsky and Gregory Corso (essays which became part of *Lonesome Traveler*). He broke up with Dodie in 1959 and *Doctor Sax* came out to yet more bad reviews as did *Maggie Cassidy* and *Mexico City Blues* later that year. As this work pattern indicates, Kerouac repeatedly managed to pull out of his drink problems to get down to periods devoted to what Holmes called the 'day-to-day routines' of writing—a capacity that Holmes felt did not receive sufficient emphasis—especially in Kerouac's own accounts.[85] Yet, having noted this, it must also be added that this ability to pull out of alcohol-dependence to get on with his writing was always declining.

Ironically, however, 1959 saw Kerouac's most unqualified critical success during his lifetime. Unlikely enough, this was *Pull My Daisy*, which won an award at the San Francisco Film festival and ran for two weeks in New York, albeit to largely empty auditoriums. Kerouac's spontaneous narration attracted substantial critical praise, and the film featured Larry Rivers as Neal Cassady, Gregory Corso as Kerouac, Allen Ginsberg and Peter Orlovsky as themselves and Delphine Seyrig as Carolyn Cassady.

Kerouac crashed around New York for much of 1959 though he did travel to San Francisco to collect the prize awarded to *Pull My Daisy*. He was by now more and more often out of control, falling down twice at the award ceremony, for example. Yet he continued to give readings and make recordings, despite the fact that his alcohol over-use and increasing heroin abuse were dismantling him steadily. He was becoming more religious at this time and (intermittently) rather racist. He did also do a little writing: he expanded 'Lucien Midnight' (now *Old Angel Midnight*)—the new sections appearing eventually in *Evergreen Review*.

Old Angel Midnight is perhaps best described as a species of prose poem written over a number of years. It consists of sixty-seven relatively short, often semi-autonomous sections (some sections are very short and some clearly interrelate). Overall, though, the work is unified by its over-arching commitment to literary and linguistic experimentation. In a letter to John Clellon Holmes Kerouac called it 'automatic writing',[86] but this label is somewhat misleading. It is not what Yeats or the surrealists had in mind so much as Kerouac writing without any attempt to 'censor or alter his expression'[87] and paying close attention to language shapes and—above all—sounds. Many sections are stimulated by listening and responding to sounds heard 'through the window' (5). This window is both physical—the window next to which he wrote the poetry, and mental—a window of consciousness.

Old Angel Midnight was mostly written in a cabin in the hills behind San Francisco overlooking the city, though a couple of sections were composed in the city itself. *Old Angel Midnight* records not only the sounds the writer hears and (sometimes) the sights he sees, but also their impact upon his mind. He appears to be, in part, 'Old Angel Midnight': 'I ... had Old Angel Midnight for my name' (1). But he predominantly seems to be 'John Kerouac transliterator' (30). A dialogue exists between these different aspects of the writer,[88] as he strives to find a language able to record his impressions. Thus onomatopoeia is used to try to convey the actual sounds heard. But even more often textual allusions invoke past writers and their varied attempts to convey impressions and meanings. James Joyce is the principle past master summoned up, but also (in Kerouac's words, 'Dostopoffsy ... Balzac in *Cousine Bette* ... Tristram Shraundy Shern, marvelous book ... Elmer Payo Robinson, the author of Oogoon and Shmarl Baudelaire ... Ole Hornshaw too the Gerst poetizer, with Ilium and Troy ... Philip Whalen ... Schneider ... Allen O Shinzberg ... Mayo Opo Waldo Elmo Poe ... Hawthorn ... Melville ... Brooklyn Bridge and John Holmes ... (the aunorthist not the noet)' (28; all spellings in the original). This curiously spelt list of influences indicates how Kerouac playfully uses puns, allusions and word-play as well as language-sounds to convey his meanings. The writing is plainly not always as spontaneous as it appears, though much is composed with an improvisational 'bop' freedom, using free-form word-associations.[89] Kerouac fully recognizes that his project—to communicate 'the sounds of the universe coming through my window'—cannot isolate itself from the many other sounds in his head. An enormous variety of voices, some literary, some more mundane, echo in his mind. Buddhist sages, haikus, the songs of birds, the sound of traffic, join up to compete with a panoply of styles, from that of Shakespeare through Joyce and other modernists, in an endless dance.

Kerouac noted on the book's back cover that he regarded *Old Angel Midnight* as 'the only book I've ever written in which I allow myself the right to say anything I want, absolutely and positively anything', which seems to point the reader towards a work of the most complete authenticity. Yet, once more, the result is a text in which, precisely, authenticity is constantly problematized, in which identity cannot be neatly stabilized and packaged up, and where language becomes slippery and untrustworthy. *Old Angel Midnight* is literally unfathomable, as meanings proliferate. It is not an easy text to read but if its swift torrent of words is followed, an unfolding dance of meanings results and can be enjoyed. Yet underneath there also seems to be a submerged anxiety—as if Kerouac senses that language-meanings are for ever elusive, always just evading him. Perhaps this is why his later works generally become less ambitiously experimental.

Aside from the curious if sometimes compelling experimentation of 'Old Angel Midnight', and a monthly column contributed to *Escapade* which often consisted of writing from earlier in Kerouac's career (including parts of *Visions of Cody*), new writing—such as work on *Desolation Angels*—was making little progress. Talk of doing a novel about Lucien Carr remained only talk. Though he formed a new relationship with Lois Sorrells, things in New York were reaching some sort of dead end. At about this time, symptomatically, he sold the house in Northport in order to move his mother back to Florida. This did not work out. Domestic problems with Nin and her husband in Florida caused Mémêre to return to Northport, so Kerouac purchased another house there. At this time he was also being harassed because of a government- and media-sponsored belief that the 'beat generation' was un-American, even Communistic—as enshrined in the label the media applied in 1958 to those they regarded as members of the Beat Generation: *beatniks*—thus associating the Beats with Soviet Russia, which had launched the first sputnik into space in October 1957.[90] This development helped fuel Kerouac's alcohol-induced paranoia, as he angrily rejected any such charge and distanced himself from Ginsberg's increasing radicalism to prove his point.

In November 1957 Kerouac left New York briefly, first to take part in a 'Steve Allen Plymouth Show' reading in Hollywood, and then on to San Francisco where he stayed in Hyphen-House with Philip Whalen, mixing with a new group of writers including Lew Welch, Jay Blaise and Albert Saijo. After the usual round of lionizations and drunkenness, he was driven back to New York by Welch, en route writing *Trip-Trap: Haiku Along the Road from San Francisco* with Welch and Saijo.

In New York Kerouac resumed his familiar, almost constant, round of debauchery. Consequently, though *Mexico City Blues* was published in October 1959, *Maggie Cassidy* in December 1959, and *Excerpts from Visions of Cody* in that same month (in the New Directions edition of only 750 copies), new writing had almost dried up. He was entering another barren spell: attempts to restart *Desolation Angels* kept stalling. Lois Sorrells was now living with him (unusually, permitted to do so by Mémêre who generally sought to exclude Kerouac's female friends from the house). Though in poor condition because of his alcoholism, Kerouac managed to see into print a string of publications during 1960. These,

The cover design for the first edition of *Maggie Cassidy*, 1959.

however, were once again largely not the result of new writing, but past work. Apart from a variety of pieces in anthologies, these publications included his long poem, 'Rimbaud' in *Yugen*, his Buddhist reflections, *The Scripture of the Golden Eternity* with Yugen Press, and *Tristessa* and *Lonesome Traveler*. This last publication collected together Kerouac's shorter writings.

Lonesome Traveler consists of either heavily autobiographical short stories or highly personalized journalism—such as 'New York Scenes', first published by Holiday in 1959, and 'The Vanishing American Hobo', also published by Holiday. Kerouac's personalized journalism reads somewhat like what would be later christened 'factionalism'—journalism so heavily reworked and so based in personal experiences as to fictionalize the report. These short works were taken from writing spanning almost the whole of the 1950s: an account of how Kerouac failed to get signed on as a member of Cru's ship in 1951, entitled 'Piers of the Homeless Night' and another, 'Mexico Fellaheen', about his early experiences in Mexico—both perhaps reworked 'out-takes' from the sprawling expansion of *On the Road*'s near-endless re-draftings in the first seven years of the 1950s; 'The Railroad Earth', drawing on his experiences as a brakeman in San Francisco; 'Slobs of the Kitchen Sea', about his experiences on the *SS Carruth*; and 'Alone on a Mountain Top', describing his fire-watching duties on Desolation Peak in the Cascades in 1956. Of uneven quality, *Lonesome Traveler* does however also showcase some fine spontaneous writing, particularly in the early pages of 'The Railroad Earth', which constitutes the centerpiece of the collection. *Lonesome Traveler*'s real importance perhaps resides in how it suggested to others a way of re-approaching the art of personal reportage—a suggestion supported by the way that, later, New Journalists like Hunter S. Thompson plainly drew some inspiration form Kerouac's unique style of reportage.

Just at this moment, as Kerouac's health was disintegrating even more, severely impeding his ability to write, several publication opportunities fell his way in quick succession. Lawrence Ferlinghetti agreed after all to bring out a selection taken from *The Book of Dreams* as a City Lights book, and arrived in New York from San Francisco to help sort out this (and other) manuscripts. He and Kerouac became friendly and

Ferlinghetti offered the use of his Big Sur cabin in Bixby Canyon south of San Francisco. Ferlinghetti's intention was to provide Kerouac with a retreat where he could sober up.

Kerouac traveled west to take up Ferlinghetti's offer and, after launching out on a massive binge in San Francisco with Whalen, he journeyed by bus and taxicab to Bixby Canyon (see ***Big Sur***). There he wrote a long sound-poem, 'Sea' (eventually printed as an appendix to *Big Sur*), but could not settle in the cabin and returned to drunken bingeing in San Francisco with Welch. There he met up with the Cassadys, drank some more, met up with the Cassadys again, drank even more, returned with his fellow bingers to Bixby Canyon, binged yet again, returned to San Francisco, and there met another of Cassady's other women, Jacky Gibson. In the midst of this appalling alcoholic spiral, Jacky and Kerouac somehow formed a relationship and planned marriage, though the relationship was far from stable. They retired to Bixby Canyon via the Cassadys' house, but Kerouac was now in such personal chaos that everything disintegrated (as retold in ***Big Sur***). He fled back to San Francisco and from there returned to Mémêre in Northport.

The dustcover of *Lonesome Traveler* (1960), featuring a sketch by Larry Rivers.

He was still suffering from writer's block, though he did see through the publication of *Rimbaud* and *The Book of Dreams*—both published to almost total critical silence. Early 1961 saw him under new legal threats from Joan Haverty for maintenance (after she had divorced her new husband). His bisexuality was now more pronounced: Lois Sorrells, with whom he had re-connected, often found him in Ginsberg's bed at this time. He tried psilocybin with Ginsberg at Timothy Leary's clinic and generally blundered chaotically around in New York until a flare-up of phlebitis precipitated a move back to his mother, whom he had earlier helped move back to Florida.

From Florida he flew to Mexico City and labored for a month on *An American Passed Here*. Intended to be a separate piece of fiction, it later became the last half of *Desolation Angels*. The manuscript needed to be worked on for a long time after this start, but it marked a return to creativity. He also launched out on some fairly risky, chaotic, drink-fuelled escapades, and eventually retreated, exhausted, to Florida. Soon, however, somewhat recharged, he returned to New York to attend a paternity hearing over Joan's daughter, Jan (he never accepted this paternity though Jan was indeed his daughter). He met up with Corso and then returned to Orlando. Later that year, using benzedrine, he wrote *Big Sur* in ten nights on a big roll of teletype paper—so returning to the technique he had used when composing *On the Road*.

Big Sur traces the exploits, thoughts and feelings of a narrator, Jack Duluoz, in the grip of a series of mental disruptions induced by alcohol. Duluoz is depicted as careering out of control, as he experiences ever more severe bouts of delirium tremens each time he comes to the end of a drinking binge in a prolonged alternation of over-drinking and attempted abstinence during the six-week period spanned by the book. A friend, Lorenz Monsanto, has offered him the use of an isolated cabin in Raton Canyon, Big Sur to sober up. Duluoz travels West to take up this offer, yet, instead of quietly slipping off to the cabin, he instead broadcasts his arrival in San Francisco, so precipitating an enormous drinking binge. He finally makes it to Monsanto's cabin, but stays only briefly and returns to San Francisco—a pattern repeated twice more. On each occasion he cannot bear to remain in Raton Canyon for more than a short time. A famous writer, 'the bloody "King of the Beatniks"' (4), Duluoz is widely fêted—the reluctant spokesman for a youth cult. Consequently, he cannot confidently distinguish friends from hangers on, as both seek him out to socialize. He is all too readily lured out on drunken binges, and on one of these a woman called Billie Dabney becomes a companion. She is the lover of Duluoz's closest friend, Cody (though recently Jack and Cody have drifted apart whilst Cody was in jail on a drugs offence). Cody is, however, already married—to Evelyn, a woman whom he once 'shared' with Duluoz. Since Cody therefore cannot devote sufficient time and attention to Billie to ensure their affair endures, he passes her over to Duluoz—in a tension-laden gesture recapitulating past, ambiguously shared intimacies.

Billie has a child, Elliot, from a former relationship, who Duluoz feels constantly hampers his forming a relationship with Billie, particularly when she lets Elliot watch their love-making. Though Duluoz recognizes that he is 'jealous' of the attention Billie gives the child, he cannot stop making it clear he dislikes Elliot, which Billie finds stressful. This predicament—her treatment at the hands of Cody and her endeavors to cope with Duluoz's moody alcoholism and mental instability--finally reduces her to total distress. Near the novel's end, Duluoz describes how, barely coherent, she frantically digs a garbage-pit in Raton Canyon about the size and shape of a child's coffin, to his eyes exactly the same size as Elliot. Yet all this is Duluoz's interpretation: only the night before, he was in the grip of severe hallucinations which kept him sleepless and literally raving all night. Consequently we are unsure of his mental state and whether what he describes is accurate, not least because he tells us, 'I realize everybody is just living their lives quietly but it's only me that's insane' (156). The novel stylistically replicates Duluoz's experiences as he slips in and out of the waking hallucinations of delirium tremens.

To convey Duluoz's loss of control the style constantly skids between present and past tenses, often inter-cut with brief excursions backwards and forwards in memory. This mirrors the 'skidding' occurring in Duluoz's mind as he degenerates during the six-week period that the novel covers. Significantly in this respect, use of the present-tense increasingly dominates the narrative though the tense-changes always seem slightly out of control. *Big Sur* becomes a nakedly caustic representation of an individual's decline.[91]

From first 'groaning from another drinking bout' (3) to last, the novel also depicts the thoughts and feelings of an individual in the process of recognizing his consequent mental disintegration. The novel's spatial structure enhances this process, with each of Duluoz's three descents down into Rayon Canyon representing a deeper descent into a personal hell of delirium tremens. *Big Sur* is a harrowing read, particularly in the light of Kerouac's own life—making it one of his most truly autobiographical novels. Indeed Kerouac himself regarded *Big Sur* as 'honester' than all his other books up to this point.

Having completed his *Big Sur* typing marathon, Kerouac rapidly drank most of a case of cognac and ended up in hospital. He followed this with a long drunken spell in New

York. Only Lucien Carr out of his circle of old friends was still around and still friendly. He returned to Orlando and retyped *Big Sur* in December 1961 to render it amenable to publication.

Chapter Six: Endings

Kerouac was now a very long way down the spiral of excessive drug and alcohol consumption that had begun as World War Two drew to its close. There was to be no going back. Though at this point—to Kerouac's delight, for the book was one of his favorites—*Visions of Gerard* was finally accepted for publication, he was deeply unsettled. Periodically, he left Mémêre in Orlando to go on drunken binges. Mostly he drank heavily at home. He visited John Clellon Holmes, revisited Lowell, and then returned to Florida via New York. His mother had meanwhile decided they needed to return to New York State, and he traveled to Northport to look for a house, buying one later in 1962. *Big Sur* was published, and he now started on a new novel, *Vanity of Duluoz*, drawing together much of the material left over from the 'Duluoz legend' in what amounted to a mopping up operation.

The dustcover of *Visions of Gerard*, 1962. Kerouac ensured this book was particularly beautifully produced.

His problematic relationship with Mémêre intensified. He began to cut off other contacts, corresponding only with Clellon Holmes, Lois Sorrells and Ed White; yet he was still drinking heavily, even when he stayed at home. He wrote a little—chiefly revising *Visions of Gerard* for publication. Neal Cassady visited him briefly. He still sought sexual liaisons but by now was almost entirely sexually dysfunctional, whether with women or men. He visited John Clellon Holmes again, then returned to Lowell in September 1962, but his drunkenness created constant problems for him wherever he was.

After moving back to Northport in November 1962 Kerouac continued work on *Vanity of Duluoz*. But he was becoming more and more deeply misogynistic in his behavior, and increasingly prone to racism. As Vietnam and the women's liberation movement brewed up, so Kerouac's world-view became more and more anachronistic. Despite going on the wagon for a while, his alcohol-fuelled degeneration accelerated in 1963. The fate of *Visions of Gerard* did not help. Despite particularly fine production standards, hostile reviews predominated when it was published in September 1963, precipitating further drinking. A disastrous reading at Harvard followed in March 1964. However, in the Summer of 1964 he started writing again, continuing *Vanity of Duluoz* and expanding *Old Angel Midnight*. He also re-wrote both the long worked-over *Desolation Angels* and the more recent *An American Passed Here*, written in Mexico (the latter to become, soon afterwards, the 'Passing Through' sections of *Desolation Angels* at the behest of its publishers). This marked the prelude to the book's completion.

The dustcover of the first edition of *Desolation Angels* (1965).

Desolation Angels consists of a series of trips. First, its narrator, Jack Duluoz, journeys to Seattle, San Francisco, Mexico City and New York (from where he visits Washington, his mother and sister in North Carolina, and William Carlos Williams in Paterson). Next he moves on to Tangiers (to visit Bull Hubbard), and then Paris and London. From London he returns to America—first to New York, and then to Florida, where his mother has moved. Next he travels with his mother to California and back to Florida before revisiting Mexico and finally New York. On these journeys Duluoz recurrently links up with three poets, Irwin Garden, Raphael Urso and Simon Darlovsky. He finally christens these three his 'Desolation Angels' (366).

On these trips Duluoz details the people he meets, the things he does and the drugs and alcohol he consumes. This more or less chaotic story is narrated with pace, energy and humor.[92] However, its opening has a darker side. This depicts Duluoz working as a fire-lookout in the Cascades. Recalling this period 'five years later' (345), he speaks of this Desolation Peak fire-watching period as a '"turningabout"', 'turning from a youthful brave sense of adventure to a complete nausea' (305). The cause of this is his isolation: 'no liquor, no drugs, no chance of faking it but face to face with ole Hateful Duluoz' (30). He wavers between contemplative fulfilment and feelings of boredom and self-hatred, and ends up close to breakdown: 'I could go mad in this' (35). His account of his decline on Desolation Peak is marked by increasingly disrupted language and syntax, as he reaches a pitch of 'abysmal nothingness ... my mind's in rags' (83).

Duluoz links this movingly wretched 'turningabout' to another, later one, experienced in Tangiers as a result of an opium overdose. But this second 'nausea concerning experience' in Tangiers (305) is very different from the abysmal depths plumbed in the Cascades: 'on the opium overdose I felt snarling dreary thoughts about ... the world—all I wanted now was Wheaties by a pine breeze kitchen ... a vision of my childhood in America' (320). This attempt to link two 'turningabouts' reads like a search for some pattern to his adventures, especially as the second coincides with a sentimental resolve to return 'home' (308).[93] And Duluoz does indeed go back to America, where he sets up home with his mother. Enacting this sentimental dream is, however, quite distinct from his prolonged self-analysis on Desolation Peak. On his fire-watch he had scorned 'a discarded cowboy book ... full of sentimentality and long-winded comments' (57)—a scorn that now serves as an ironic verdict upon Jack's garrulous reflections about his love for his mother and his despair with the world. The keenness of his self-critique has dissipated. Simply put, he has deteriorated sharply.

The book has powerful moments, particularly on Desolation Peak and when Duluoz first dives back into American society in Seattle. But *Desolation Angels* is obviously two novels more or less spliced together, and 'Passing Through', the one mostly composed second (originally called 'An American Passed Here') is less penetrative and convincing, as Duluoz becomes preoccupied with wrestling with his own status as a media personality and the 'mess' that results because he cannot handle either his fame or the accompanying public scrutiny. He becomes ever more self-regarding, and his journeying increasingly consists merely of curt descriptions of 'Passing Through'. Though an astute critique of the mendacity of media celebrity-promotion is established, the fact that the first-person narrator has a very particular identity (a fêted Beat poet and novelist) deprives the text of wider social resonance. Near the end, this shift of focus is defined by Duluoz's self-assessment. To begin with, he offers the sort of contradiction-ridden identity of earlier novels' narrators, if pitched in a newly self-aggrandizing way: 'I'm a French-Canadian Iroquois American aristocratic Breton Cornish democrat'. But now he adds 'or even a Beat hipster' (334). The way that some sort of break is involved in assuming this last identity ('or even') marks out this text as different: more self-obsessed, more transient: shallowly passing over rather than penetrating to a core—and even accepting the media's compartmentalization of him.

At this time, Kerouac's mother sold the Northport house and they together moved back to St. Petersburg in Florida (1964). His sister died shortly after breaking up with her husband, further depressing Kerouac. After extensive editing work, *Desolation Angels* was accepted for publication but was reviewed badly on its release in May 1965.

Just prior to *Desolation Angels*' publication, Kerouac made a brief trip to France: to Paris and then Brittany, writing out an account of his trip on his return (see ***Satori in Paris***).

Satori in Paris is a garrulous, first-person account of its narrator's brief visit to France. It opens by proposing that the visit precipitated a 'satori' and proposes a series of possible moments when this may have occurred (the satori in question is a Zen satori—an illumination or enlightenment in one's state of consciousness).94 But the list of various incidents on his French travels identified by the first-person narrator as possibly providing the '"sudden illumination"' or '"sudden awakening"' (7) seem relatively insignificant. Instead they constitute lightweight anecdotes, despite the title's sonorous promise of enlightenment.95

Satori in Paris therefore becomes a rather inconclusive account of the inconsequential adventures of the narrator: in Paris for a few days, on a train ride to Brest (meaning to fly there, he misses his plane), then during two-days in Brest and on a train ride back to Paris, and finally during a taxi-ride to Orly airport. The narrator meets and converses quite fluently with a number of French people.96 But gradually he becomes disenchanted with France, especially when his amateurish attempts to carry out genealogical research are stymied by unhelpful librarians. He becomes increasingly disillusioned with the people he meets because of their frequently abrupt treatment of him. By the end he expects them to behave in this way, like a 'thin nosed sonumbitch in Paris-est-Pourri shit' (116). This is not to say that he does not meet some friendly French people; he certainly does. But he ends up all too happy to be flying back to his home in Florida: 'I'se ready' (113).

Yet, in large part the dismissive treatment he experiences can be seen to be his fault. He constantly fails to communicate politely with the people he meets, and the text relates this to his unremitting drunkenness. His misadventures are inextricably linked to his bouts of inebriation. The nadir of this carefully recorded drunken progress is reached when he enters the home of a French family bearing the same name as his mother (Lebris). These poor unfortunates have to put up with him requisitioning large shots from 'a huge bottle of cognac' (94): 'I even went so far as to help myself, to myself's invitation (but with a polite (?) eh?)', the narrator explains, half-apologetically (102). This decline soon leads to Kerouac scrambling to leave France.

The narrator recognizes that his failure to communicate successfully is also related to cultural differences that he sometimes manages—briefly—to bridge: 'what a miracle are different languages .... That people actually understand what their tongues are babbling. And that eyes do shine to understand, and that responses are made' (46-47). But, overall, his case seems hopeless. He increasingly realizes that any attainment of understanding and self-understanding lies beyond him. He seems culturally adrift. The fact his visit to France is partly a search for an identity is indicative of how he is far from comfortable with his existing characterization as a famous writer. He hopes his genealogical researches will reveal him to be a Breton aristocrat. That this search fails serves as a satiric commentary on these pretensions. At the end, the only hope seems to be for divine intervention.

This bleak portrait must be abstracted from what at first seems a rather over-indulgent text. But this very self-servingness is also indicative of the state of the narrator. The text offers the pathology of an alcoholic. Its disorderliness underlines its themes. The book also, with ironic humor, recognizes the narrator's failure to identify what the book's title claims to be a satori. The novella, or, perhaps, first-person journalism (the narrator is called Kerouac) implicitly accepts that 'Kerouac' has passed a point beyond which recovery is plausible—so ramming home the bleakness of his condition. Satori in Paris, for all its slightness, is a better, more comical text than first appears; its failure to provide enlightenment is part of its point.

In a sense, despite its depressing theme of alcoholism, working on *Satori in Paris* represented an escape from the claustrophobia of home life with Mémêre and the constant attention in the local Florida bars that his fame brought him (and that he brought on himself through his self-promotion). During 1965 he still occasionally left Florida on brief trips to visit Lowell (more than once), Boston, and elsewhere. Perhaps these trips made him feel rather isolated in Florida, for he moved back to New England (to Hyannis on Cape Cod).

Photograph by Allen Ginsberg of Jack Kerouac, 'Probably 104 E 5 Street ... 1964 Fall'.

1966 saw both the release of *Satori in Paris* and continued attempts by Kerouac to get *Some of the Dharma* and *Visions of Cody* published by appealing to both Grove Press and Ferlinghetti for help. The same cycle he had gone through in Florida now set in, as he began to make long, lugubrious, drunken phonecalls to a small circle of remaining friends. He did, however, manage to do some work on *Vanity of Duluoz*. Then, in September, Mémêre had a heart-attack and he needed to nurse her. He also needed money, and a drunken trip to Italy to earn some ensued, whilst Stella Sampas from Lowell moved into his house to nurse his mother. On his return from Italy he married Stella, and moved to Lowell. Stella looked after Mémêre there, but Jack was deeply depressed, a product of his remorseless over-drinking. Visitors to him, including Allen Ginsberg and Timothy Leary, generally regretted making the effort. A visit to New York with Cassady by Kerouac to meet with Ginsberg, Corso and Ken Kesey, and to see Kesey's bus, 'Further', which Neal at the time was driving for Kesey's Pranksters, developed into a morose whisky-sodden episode. In Lowell, however, Kerouac still managed to work, since Stella provided a measure of undervalued stability. *Vanity of Duluoz* was contracted (1967), finished (1967) and published (1968) in this period.

Vanity of Duluoz traces the development of Jack Duluoz. A bright, enthusiastic boy, and brilliant footballer, Jack wins a sports scholarship and, as a consequence, moves away from his French-Canadian culture into an alien world, where 'most' of the students 'are very rich' (31). Though the football team does include other sports scholarship boys, Duluoz, harboring ambitions to be a writer, feels he fits in nowhere. At Columbia College these problems persist. The resulting tensions are neatly skewered by the way Duluoz's failure to hold a place on the team is related to his lack of commitment to football, as he becomes attracted to an adolescent acting-out of a romantic bohemian lifestyle. His failure to fit in inwardly divides Duluoz, giving him a distaste for regulation. This causes confrontations with his football coaches and stems from his romantic over-valuation of individual genius, but it is also bound up with his difficulty in handling the contradictions in his life. So, on leaving Columbia and joining the merchant marines, he finds more problems. His bookishness isolates him from the crew of the ship he sails in and makes him the target of bullying. He is called up into the navy, but his dismissal from service becomes the book's key point of rupture. He walks off a parade ground in protest against over-regimentation, and is discharged after psychiatric assessment.

Sidelined from the war effort, Duluoz instead turns to a writing career, becoming involved with a circle of New York bohemians. But once again he integrates poorly, since 'they all came from well-to-do families' (222). Duluoz again shifts uneasily between attraction and repulsion. His unease climaxes when he is arrested after a killing: the unrequited homosexual attraction by one of his bohemian friends, Mueller, for another, Claude, leads to the latter murdering the former, from fear of assault. Duluoz is arrested as an accessory and briefly imprisoned. This drives him to marry his girlfriend, to raise bail. But he has been unsettled by his experiences (first when identifying Mueller's body, then on meeting the prison's inmates) and is increasingly alienated.

A passage soon after—in which he is represented as accidentally 'flashing' his penis in front of the Capitol in Washington—is symbolic: 'during the day some work's torn off the front part of my pants, I have to hold them together or my thing'll wave. As I see the Nation's Capitol, the American flag ... I whip back for my pint in backpocket ... and the thing comes out and waves at the American flag and the Capitol' (115-16). This symbolizes how Duluoz always seems both misplaced and nakedly exposed. But he fails to draw coherent conclusions from the complex interactions of class, ethnicity, and sexuality which he embodies. Rather he resorts to reflex denunciations of Communism, drawing on a dominant Cold War rhetoric which places him, paradoxically, in allegiance with a mainstream within which he otherwise fits poorly (12, 85). It is therefore ironic that he believes he is under government surveillance: 'I've always had the feeling the FBI was watching me' (263). There is an unstable incoherence at the core of Duluoz's responses—a paranoia rooted in either illusion or reality—matching the paranoid atmosphere of fifties' America.

Vanity of Duluoz's narrative succeeds in being both complex yet unsatisfying in its portrait of the USA's progress from the Depression of the early forties through World War Two into fifties' prosperity. The narrator defends yet also seems deeply alienated from an '"America" that has become such a potboiler of broken convictions, messes of rioting and fighting in the streets, hoodlumism, cynical administration ... grandeur all gone in the mosaic mesh of Television' (106). A repressive weariness of tone increasingly bears down upon Duluoz's narrative.

By the time *Vanity of Duluoz* was published, Kerouac was drinking copiously, prodigiously. The book's bad reviews made matters worse. A few drunken excursions out of Lowell took place, including one to Quebec for a television interview, which reveals well the state he was now in: as the TV program's presenter, Bernard Séguin explained, 'he oscillated between panic and anger and ... went off to seek an argument in some tavern'.[97] Soon after this he also gave a revealing and significant *Paris Review* interview (with Ted Berrigan, Aram Saroyan and Duncan McNaughton in 1967). Then Neal Cassady died, to Kerouac's distress, in early 1968, but his drinking could hardly increase much more. Mémêre wanted to move back to Florida, and to finance this move, Kerouac sold many of his letters, also putting up the Lowell house and Hyannis, Cape Cod, for sale. Though he traveled to Germany and later appeared on William F. Buckley's show, 'Firing Line', in September 1968 during one of his occasional excursions out of Lowell, his public appearances were increasingly difficult and rare. His 'Firing Line' appearance, for example, was a debacle during which, drunk, he was carved apart by Buckley's rapier wit.

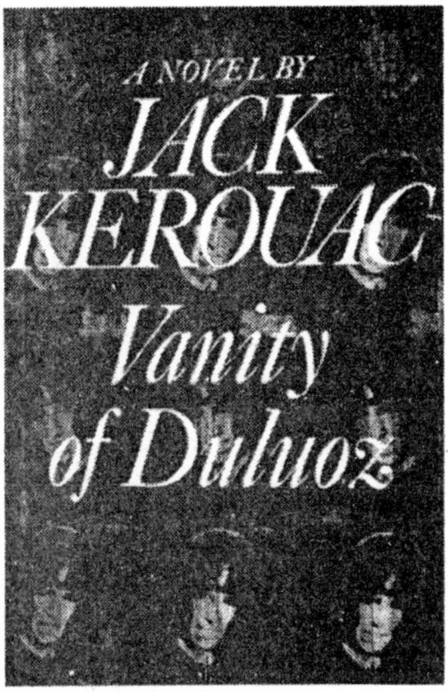

Dustcover design for Kerouac's *Vanity of Duluoz* (1968).

His move back to St. Petersburg in 1968 was his final one. He had become addicted to dexedrine which he used to control the side effects of his drinking. Secretly he was planning to divorce Stella. At this time, there was little sign of just how famous he and his writings were destined to become. He was living in relative poverty, and though he always kept his papers in apple-pie order he could never have imagined that in 2001 his scroll typescript of *On the Road* would be destined to sell for well over two million dollars.

He was still striving to get *Visions of Cody* published, making plaintive phone calls to Ferlinghetti on the West Coast.[98] The only 'writing' he could manage in 1969 was to piece together *Pic* from previous writing, recasting the pieces and reworking some in African-American Southern dialect.

Pic takes as its narrator Pictorial Review Jackson—a ten-year-old African. His story begins in North Carolina when his mother dies and his brother leaves home. Orphaned, Pic is left with his paternal grandfather, who also dies, leaving Pic to be taken in by his Aunt Gastonia. There is some resistance to this, partly from her husband, Uncle Sim, but mostly from Pic's maternal grandfather, Grandpa Jelkey. In the past, Pic's father blinded Grandpa Jelkey. The latter, motivated by revenge, therefore lays a curse on Pic. Terrified, the boy falls ill. Fortunately, his elder brother, Slim, unexpectedly returns, and after some argument, sneaks back at night to whisk Pic off to New York. The bus ride is carefully described, as is a brief period in New York where Slim lives with a woman called Sheila who has just lost her job. The next day Slim obtains work in a cookie factory but the labor gives him cramps and he is signed off. That same evening he is offered a jazz-gig in a nightclub but is again laid off afterwards. The couple decides to spend Sheila's savings traveling to California where Sheila's sister now lives. Since Sheila is pregnant and they are too broke for all three to travel by train, Slim and Pic hitch-hike. However, they find lifts difficult to obtain and after a few adventures are offered jobs in a Catholic Church in Pittsburgh, Slim as a janitor and Pic as a cantor. As soon as they have saved enough for the rest of the journey, they catch a Greyhound to Sacramento Valley and meet up with Sheila.

The story's obvious links to *The Adventures of Huckleberry Finn* are underlined by the dialect voice in which Pic tells his story. The prose account also often resounds with the rhythms of the blues. It has a light rapidity that is appealing, if not always wholly convincing.[99] The book amounts to a picaresque adventure: any quest is simply for a situation where a roof can be secured and a living can be earned. The novella breaks off before this is achieved though California has, conventionally enough, been set up as a promised land offering Pic and Slim delivery from hardship. Such conventional sentimentalism recurs throughout *Pic*, though this is partly offset by the text's depictions of poverty.

Pic also founders somewhat on its slightly stereotypical portrait of its African-Americans, Pic and Slim, whose talents—predictably—reside in their musical abilities (Slim's horn-blowing, Pic's singing). It remains a patchy text, pieced together from fragments of earlier writings. But some passages have a real power—particularly its portrait of Times Square, where a prophet of doom denounces television's pernicious influence. The book also bears a potent message about the way post-war America deploys a network of lines—color-lines, production lines, television lines—repressively crisscrossing the USA.

Kerouac was still writing, completing an article, 'After Me, the Deluge', and planned a further novel about his father. But his condition was terminal: on October 21, 1969, he died in hospital from haemorrhaging caused almost certainly by his alcoholism.

Coda

During this debilitating life of ever-increasing substance and alcohol abuse, Kerouac brought into being, with the 1951 *On the Road* scroll, a new writing voice—conveyed in what is termed, somewhat misleadingly, 'spontaneous prose'—and developed it, for better and often for worse, in over a dozen novels, as well as short stories, poems and articles. In this process, Kerouac melded together the popular and the 'literary' as he strove to negotiate thematic and stylistic ways to portray individuals seeking to escape, evade or cope with the amorphous thrashings of change in post-1945, Cold War American society. He was constantly seeking to find ways to depict the often damaging impact of this society, which was growing rapidly more affluent for many but in ways that could swiftly alienate those who remained poor and leave them writhing in the often unsympathetic grip of processes of increasing post-war commercialization that many Americans could not, and generally did not wish to, resist. Visions of Cody's depiction of a stoned Duluoz trying to interpret a kaleidoscope of reflections in a cafeteria window stands as a type of symptomatic passage:

> An immense plate glass window in this white cafeteria ... faces the street (Sixth Avenue) but with inside neon tubular lights reflected in the window and they in turn illuminating the ... walls which are therefore also reflected and hang in the street with the tubular neons ...
>
> But now let's examine it closer. Riddled and penetrated and obscured and rippled and haunted and of course like kaleidoscope over kaleidoscope but above the glittering street are the darkened or brown-lit windows of Sixth Avenue semi-

> flophouses and beat doll shops and blackdust plumbing shops and Waldorf Cafeteria Employment Office closed, red neons through windows at other end—Furthest up in dark is the focus of this entire human scene: this is a fourth floor unwashed window with the shade not drawn more than a foot but ever so thin brown filthy lace or muslin curtain (and now the light went off!!) failing to hide the shadow of a iron bed. Now that it's gone off the mirror pillar is suddenly revealed all the way to its entire length because my attention had been on the actual window and the reflected pillar was just barely touching the edge of the window and I didn't know it. Most amazing of all now this reflected mirror pillar hanging in the street is at the same time reflecting the tubular neon, the real one inside, not the imagined one, outside ... (*VC*, 16-17)

This sort of multi-faceted, pulsing sense of modernity's passage towards new, post-war commodification and divisions of wealth (white cafeteria neons interlaced with filthy muslin curtains) is why, despite continuing institutional skepticism, his works continue to be read and remain in print.

One of Kerouac's key achievements is to have explored the grey area that lies between autobiography, fact, and fiction in this modern world—the triangulation set up between the three and the way that autobiography, as it necessarily becomes confessional storytelling, traverses between the other two. As Kerouac grew older and his fame also grew, this exploration became increasingly self-conscious. The issues became how to deal with fame and celebrity, and how the processes of media attention—his media lionization—generated an ever more severe crisis for a writer engaged in a search for authenticity. It is in his sharp perception of the way that writing-asreporting becomes bound up with the writer's own preconceptions and the expectations of his audience that one of Kerouac's significant achievements resides. These ideas will come to lie behind the work of many succeeding writers—in their celebration or their mournful recognition of the ironic inescapability of the subjective. This can be seen particularly in the writing of many of those who became known as the New Journalists (from Hunter S. Thompson's 'gonzo' journalism at one extreme, to the growing self-reflexivity of even the most conservative of hacks at the other). Kerouac in this way is a figure whose influence on some New Journalist practices is considerable. Yet in this process existed self-destructive cycles: his failure to secure 'the pearl' in his life was, he recognized, inevitable—and perhaps this drove his destructive addictions to alcohol and drugs. His search for a 'pearl' propelled him outside of society, yet his rebellion was not securely based on a political philosophy but more on strong feeling, and on fellow feelings for mankind. So even as, for example, *On the Road* recognized the existence of a military-industrial complex, that Eisenhower at the end of his presidency denounced, the seeds also existed for his conservative withdrawal from 1960s' resistance to the Vietnam war that Allen Ginsberg embraced enthusiastically.

It is surely true that Kerouac's fiction largely draws on 'true life' events. Examining his life makes it clear that Kerouac is just as contradictory and confused, as honest and mendacious, as authentic and inauthentic as the narrators he creates. This in turn makes his writing almost uniquely honest in its excoriating revelation of sel. Kerouac offers a self-portrait sounding a plangent note of dissidence and resistance to social and personal deceit, yet somehow also a self that was increasingly unable to resist such deceit's allures. Kerouac, in his own words, always strives to adhere to 'the heartbreaking discipline of the veritable fire ordeal where you can't go back' (*DA*, 238).

Appendix A: Key to selected pseudonyms in Kerouac's writing

Abbreviations used:

The Town and the City - *TC*
And the Hippos Were Boiled in Their Tanks - *H*
On the Road - *OR*
Visions of Cody - *VC*
Doctor Sax - *DS*
Maggie Cassidy - *MC*
Lonesome Traveler - *LT*
The Subterraneans - *S*
Visions of Gerard - *VG*
Tristessa - *T*
Old Angel Midnight - *OA*
Dharma Bums - *DB*
Desolation Angels - *DA*
Big Sur - *BS*
Satori in Paris - *SP*
Vanity of Duluoz - *VD*
Pic - *P*

Names are cross-referenced. Pseudonyms appear in regular type, real names in bold.

Adams, Joan Vollmer (common law wife of Burroughs): Jane (*OR*, *S*); Mary Dennison (*TC*); June Hubbard (*VC*); June Evans (*BD*, *DA*, *VD*)
Ansen, Alan (NYC poet): Rollo Greb (*OR*); Irwin Swenson (*VC*, *BD*); Austin Bromberg (*S*)
Apostolos, George (Lowell friend): Danny (D. J.) Mulverhill (*TC*); G. J. Rigopoulos (*DS*, *MC*); G. J. Rigolopoulos (*VD*)
Arminger, Priscilla (NY friend): see Vicki Russell
Avakian, George (NY prep school friend): Chuck Derounian (*VD*)
Baily, Ginger (NYC friend and musician): Peaches Martin (*OR*, *VC*, *BD*)
Beaulieu, Henry (Lowell friend): Scotcho Rouleau (*TC*); Scotty Boldieu (*DS*); Scotcho Boldieu (*VD*)
Bertrand, Fred (Lowell friend): Vinnie Bergerac (*DS*, *MC*)
Bertrand, Happy (father of Lowell friend): Lucky Bergerac (*DS*)
Bertrand, Leona (Leo) (mother of Lowell friend): Charlie Bergerac
Blake, Paul (second husband of Caroline Kerouac): Big Luke (*DB*)
Blake, Paul Jr. (son of Caroline Kerouac): Little Luke (*DB*)
Brandenberg, Bob (NYC friend): Bob Hindenburg (*VC*, *BD*)
Brierly, Justin W. (Denver friend): Denver D. Doll (*OR*); Justin G. Mannerly (*VC*); Manley Mannerly (*BD*)
Brodie, Iris (NYC friend): Roxanne (*S*)
Buckley, William F. Jr. (NYC schoolfriend): William F. Buckley Jr. (*VD*)
Burford, Beverley (Denver/SF friend): Babe Rawlins (*OR*); Vera Buferd (*BD*)
Burford, Bob (Denver friend): Ray Rawlins (*OR*); Bill Buferd (*VC*)
Burnett, David (son of Whit Burnett): Walt Fitzpatrick (*S*)
Burnett, Whit (NY poet and friend): Bennet Fitzpatrick (*S*)
Burns, Blackie (Washington State fire lookout): Burnie Byers (*DB*); Blacky Blake (*DA*)

Burroughs, Julie (daughter of Burroughs): Dodie Lee (*OR*)
Burroughs, William Jr. (son of Burroughs): Ray Lee (*OR*)
Burroughs, William S. (writer; friend): Will Dennison (*TC; H*); Old Bull Lee (*OR*); Frank Carmody (*S*); Bull Hubbard (*VC, DS, DA, BD*); Will Holmes Hubbard (*VD*)
Cannastra, William (Bill) (NYC friend): Finistra (*VC, BD*)
Carney, Mary (Lowell friend): Mary Gilhooley (*TC*); Maggie Cassidy (*MC, VD*)
Carr, Cessa (NYC friend): Nessa Love (*VC*)
Carr, Lucien (NYC friend): Kenny Wood (TC); Phillip Tourian (H)
Cassady, Carolyn (wife of Neal Cassady, friend, lover): Camille (*OR*); Evelyn (*VC*)
Cassady, Cathy (daughter of Cassady): Emily Pomeray (*VC*); Amy Moriarty (*OR*)
Cassady, Jamie (daughter of Cassady): Gaby Pomeray (*VC*); Joanie Moriarty (*OR*)
Cassady, John Allen (son of Cassady): Timmy Pomeray (*VC*); Timmy John Pomeray (*BS*)
Cassady, Neal (friend): Dean Moriarty (*OR*); Cody Pomeray (*VC, DB, DA, BS, BD*); Leroy (*S*)
Chandler, Billy (Lowell friend): Dicky Hampshire (*TC, DS, VD*)
Chase, Haldon (Hal) (Denver/NYC friend): Chad King (*OR*); Val Hayes (*VC*); Val King (*VC*)
Chiungas, Duke (Lowell friend): Duke Gringas (*VC*); Bruno Gringas (*DS*); Telemachus Gringas (*VD*)
Coffey, Margaret (Peggy) (Lowell friend): Pauline (Moe) Cole (*MC, VD*)
Connie (SF friend): Baby (*DA*)
Corso, Gregory (poet; friend): Yuri Gligoric (*S*); Raphael Urso (*DB, DA, BD*)
Cowen, Elise (NYC friend): Barbara Lipp (*DA*)
Cru, Henri (NYC/SF friend): Remi Boncoeur (*OR*); Deni Bleu (*VC, LT, DA, BD, VD*)
Dahlenburg, Claude (SF friend): Paul (*DA*); Bud Diefendorf (*DB*)
Damion (*OR*); Julien Love (*VC, BD*); Sam Vedder (*S*); Claude de Maubris (*VD*); Julien (*DA*)
Dastou, George (Lowell friend): Ernest Berlot (*TC*)
de Angulo, Gui (SF artist): Gia Valencia (*DA*)
Diamond, David (NY friend and composer): Sylvester Strauss (*S*)
Donlin, Bob (SF friend): Rob Donnelly (*DA*)
du Peru, Peter (SF friend): Richard di Chili (*DA*)
Duncan, Robert (SF poet): Geoffrey Donald (*DA*)
Eager, Alan (sax jazz player): Roger Beloit (*S*)
Elliot, Helen (NYC friend): Ruth Erikson (*DA*)
Elvins, Kells (friend of Burroughs): Kyles Elgins (*VD*)
Ferlinghetti, Lawrence (SF poet): Lorenzo Monsanto (*BS*)
Fitzgerald, Jack (NYC writer friend): McCarthy (*VC*)
Fourchette, Jean (aka Omar Noël) (Lowell friend): Ali Zaza (*DS*); Zouzou (*TC*); Zaza Vauriselle *MC*)

Franco, Bea (friend and lover): Terry (*S*)
Gaddis, William (novelist): Harold Sand (*S*)
Garver, William (Bill) Maynard (NYC friend): Old Bull Gaines (*DA, T, BD*); Harper (*VC*)
Gibson, Eric (son of Jackie Gibson): Elliot Dabney (*BS*)
Gibson, Jackie (SF/Big Sur friend and lover): Billie Dabney (*BS*)
Gilbert, Eddie (NYC schoolfriend): Jimmy Winchel (*VD*)
Ginsberg, Allen (poet and friend): Leon Levinsky (*TC*); Irwin Garden (*VD, DA, BS, VC, BD*); Carlo Marx (*OR*); Adam Moorad (*S*); Alvah Goldbrook (*DB*)
Ginsberg, Louis (poet and father of Ginsberg): Harry Garden (*DA*)
Glassman, Joyce (NYC friend and lover): Alyce Newman (*DA*)
Gould, Stanley (NYC friend): Ross Wallenstein (*S*); Shelley Lisle (*BD*)
Gullion, Helen (Denver friend and lover): Rita Bettencourt (*OR*)
Gullion, Ruth (Denver friend): Mary Bettencourt (*OR*)
Hampshire, Dicky (Lowell friend): Billy Chandler (*DS*)
Hansen, Diane (NY friend; one of Neal Cassady's wives): Inez (*OR*); Diana (Diane) Pomeray (*VC*)
Harrington, Alan (writer; NYC friend): Hal Hingham (*OR*); Early Wallington (*BD*)
Haverty, Joan (Kerouac's second wife): Laura (*OR*); June Ogilvie (*BD*)
Heiserberg, Jarry (SF friend): Joey Rosenberg (*BS*)
Henderson, LuAnne (Cassady's first wife): Mary Lou (*OR*); Joanna Dawson (*VC*); Annie (*S*)
Hinkle, Al (Denver/SF friend): Ed Dunkel (*OR*); Slim Buckle (*VC*); Ed Buckle (*BD*)
Hinkle, Helen (friend; wife of Hinkle): Galatea Dunkel (*OR*); Helen Buckle (*VC*)
Hoffenburg, Mason (NYC friend; writer): Jack Steen (*S*)
Holmes, Jim (Denver friend of Cassady): Tom Snark (*OR*); Tom Watson (*VC*)
Holmes, John Clellon (novelist; friend): Ian MacArthur (*OR*); Balliol MacJones (*S*); John Watson (*VC*);
Huncke, Herbert (NYC friend): Junkey (*TC*); Elmer Hassel (*OR*); Huck (*VC, BD*)
Jackson, Natalie (friend, lover of Cassady): Rosie Buchanan (*DB*); Rosemarie (*DA, BS, BD*)
Jarrell, Randall (poet): Varnum Random (*DA*)
Jeffries, Frank (Denver friend): Sam Shephard (*OR*); Dave Sherman (*VC, BD*)
Kammerer, David (NYC friend): Waldo Meister (*TC*); Ramsey Allen (*H*); Dave Stroheim (*VC*); Franz Mueller (*VD*)
Kamuca, Richie (NY friend): Ricci Comucca (*S*)
Kandel, Lenore (SF poet): Ramona Swartz (*BS*)
Keck, Bill (NYC friend): Fritz Nicholas (*S*); Dick Beck (*BD*)
Kerouac, Caroline (sister): Nin (*DS, DB, MC*)

Kerouac, Gabrielle L'Evesque (aka Mémêre) (mother): Marguerite Courbet Martin (*TC*); Ange (*VD, DS*) [she is also Sal's unnamed Aunt in *OR*]
Kerouac, Gerard (brother): Gerard Duluoz (*DS, VG*); Julian Martin (*TC*)
Kerouac, Jack: Peter Martin (*TC*) [also aspects of Joe and Francis Martin]; Mike Ryko (*H*); Sal Paradise (*OR*); Jack Duluoz (*VC, DS, MC, VG, T, DA, BS, SP, VD*); Leo Percepied (*S*); Ray Smith (*DB*) [also Jack in *BD* and Jack Kerouac in *SP* and *OA*]
Kerouac, Leo Alcide (father): George Martin (*TC*); Emil Duluoz (*DS, MC, VG, VD*)
Kingsland, John (NYC friend): John Macy (*VC*); Charles Bernard (*S*); Ronald Macy (*BD*)
Komuca, Richie (West Coast jazz tenor saxophonist): Ricci Comucca
Koumentzalis, Johnny (Lowell friend): Johnny Kazarakis (*MC, VD*)
Lamantia, Philip (poet): Francis Da Pavia (*DB*); David D'Angeli (*DA*)
Landesman, Jay (NYC editor): Jay Chapman (*VC*)
LaVigne, Robert (SF artist): Guy Levesque (*DA*)
Lee, Alene (NYC friend and lover): Mardou Fox (*S*); Irene May (*BD*)
Little, Lou (Lowell football coach): Lu Libble (*MC, VD*)
Livornese, Tom (NYC musician friend): Tom Calabrese (*VC*)
Lund, Paul (friend): John Banks (*DA*)
Mailer, Norman (NYC novelist): Harvey Marker (*DA*)
Mardean (friend): Nardine (*VC*)
McClure, Michael (poet): Ike O'Shay (*DB*); Patrick McLear (*DA, BS*)
McCorkle, Locke (friend of Snyder): Sean Monahan (*DB*); Kevin McLoch (*DA*)
Melodias, Jack (Little Jack Melody) (NYC friend): Little Zagg (*VC*)
Mémêre: see Gabrielle L'Evesque Kerouac
Mercer, Jacky Gibson: see Jackie Gibson
Merrill, Robert (poet): Merrill Randall (*DA*)
Mew, Charlie (SF friend): Jimmy Low (*DA, BD*); Charley Low (*VC*)
Montgomery, John (SF friend): Henry Morley (*DB*); Alex Fairbrother (*DA*)
Moore, Brew (West Coast jazz saxophonist): Brue Moore (*DA*)
Moreland, Dusty (painter; NYC friend): Josephine (*VC, DA, BD*); Arlene Wohlstetter (*S*)
Morris, William (SF painter): Robert Browning (*BS*)
Morrissette, Charlie (Lowell bother-in-law): Jimmy Bissonette (*MC*)
Newman, Jerry (NYC friend): Danny Richman (*VC, BD*); Larry O'Hara (*S*)
Noël, Omar: see Jean Fourchette
O'Dea, Jim (Lowell friend): Timmy Clancy (*MC, MD, VD*)
Orlovsky, Peter (poet; friend; lover of Ginsberg): George (*DB*); Simon Darlovsky (*DA, BD*)
Orlovsky, Simon (friend; Orlovsky's brother): Lafcadio Orlovsky (*DA*)
Parker, Edie (Kerouac's first wife): Judie Smith (*TC*); Janie (*H*); Edna (Johnnie) Palmer (*VD*); Edna (*BD*); Elly (*VC*)

Pauline (NYC friend and lover): Lucille (*OTR*)
Perpignan, James (SF friend): Perry Yturbide (*BS*)
Rexroth, Kenneth (SF poet): Reinhold Cacoethes (*DB*)
Rosenberg, Anton (NYC friend): Julian Alexander (*S*); Gerard Rose (*BD*)
Russell, Vicki (aka Priscilla Arminger) (NYC friend): Dorie (*OR*); Vicki (*VC*)
Saijo, Albert (SF poet friend): George Baso (*BS*)
Salvas, Roland (Lowell friend): Albert (Lousy) Lauzon (*DS, MS*)
Sampas, Charles (Lowell friend): James G. Santos (*MC*)
Sampas, Sammy (Lowell friend): Alexander Panos (*TC*); Sabby Savakis (*VD*) Sebastian (*VC*); Savas (*VG*)
Sampas, Stella (Lowell friend; third wife): Stavroula Savakis [she is also the 'wifey' addressed by the narrator in *DA*]
Smith, Paul (Big Sur friend): Ron Blake (*BS*)
Snyder, Gary (San Francisco poet): Japhy Ryder (*DB*); Jerry Wagner (*DA*)
Snyder, Thea (Snyder'sister): Rhoda Ryder (*DB*)
Solomon, Carl (NYC friend): Carl Rappaport (*VC*)
Sousiox, Ed (SF jazz alto saxophonist): Ed Fournier (*OR*); Ed Laurier (*VC*)
St Louis, Red (Lowell friend): Whitey St Clair (*MC*)
Stewart, Stephanie (NYC friend): Stephanie James (*VC*)
Stringham, Ed (NYC friend): Tom Saybrook (*OR*); Al Bingham (*BD*)
Strong, Freddy (NYC jazz singer): 'the tenorman' (when singing) (*OTR*); Freddy Strange (*VC*)
Sublette, Al (SF friend): Al/Ma! Damlette (*DA, BS, T, BD*)
Temko, Allan (Denver friend): Roland Major (*OR*); Allen Minko (*VC*); Irving Minko (*BD*)
Tomson, Bill (Denver friend): Roy Johnson (*OR*); Earl Johnson (*VC*)
Tomson, Helen (wife of Tomson): Dorothy Johnson (*OR*); Helen Johnson (*VC*)
Uhl, Don (Colorado friend): Ed Wall (*OR*); Ed Wehle (*VC*)
van Meter, Peter (NYC friend): Paddy Cordavan (*S*); Buddy van Buder (*VC, BD*)
Vidal, Gore (NYC novelist): Arial Lavalina
Villanueva, Esperanza (Mexico City friend and lover): Tristessa (*T*)
Watts, Alan (SF buddhist expert): Arthur Whane (*BS*); Alex Aums (*DA*)
Weaver, Helen (NY lover): Ruth Heaper (*DA*)
Welch, Lew (SF poet): Dave Wain (*BS*)
Whalen, Philip (NYC/SF poet): Warren Coughlin (*DB*); Ben Fagan (*BS*)
White, Ed (artist; NY friend): Tim Gray (*OR*); Ed Gray (*VC*); Guy/Al Green (*BD*)
White, Phil (NYC friend): Phil Blackman (*VC*)
Williams, William Carlos (poet): Dr. Williams (*DA*)
Witt-Diamant, Ruth (SF poet): Rose Wise Lazuli (*DA*)
Wong, Victor (SF friend): Arthur Ma (*BS*)

Wyse, Seymour (NY schoolfriend): Lionel Smart (*VC, MC, BD, VD*)
Young, Céline (Columbia friend): Barbara (*H*); Cecily (*VD*)

Alexander, Julian (*S*): **Anton Rosenberg**
Allen, Ramsey (*H*): **David Kammerer**
Ange (*VD, DS*): **Gabrielle L'Evesque Kerouac**
Annie (*S*): **LuAnne Henderson**
Aums, Alex (*DA*): **Alan Watts**
Baby (*DA*): **Connie**
Banks, John (*DA*): **Paul Lund**
Barbara (*H*): **Céline Young**
Baso, George (*BS*): **Albert Saijo**
Beck, Dick (*BD*): **Bill Keck**
Beloit, Roger (*S*): **Alan Eager**
Bergerac, Charlie (*DS*): **Leona (Leo) Bertrand**
Bergerac, Lucky (*DS*): **Happy Bertrand**
Bergerac, Vinnie (*MC*): **Fred Bertrand**
Berlot, Ernest (*TC*): **George Dastou**
Bernard, Charles (*S*): **John Kingsland**
Bettencourt, Mary (*OR*): **Ruth Gullion**
Bettencourt, Rita (*OR*): **Helen Gullion**
Bingham, Al (*BD*): **Ed Stringham**
Bissonette, Jimmy (*MC*): **Charlie Morrissette**
Blackman, Phil (*VC*): **Phil White**
Blake, Blacky (*DA*): **Blackie Burns**
Blake, Ron (*BS*): **Paul Smith**
Bleu, Deni (*LT, VD, DA, BD, VC*): **Henry Cru**
Boldieu, Scotcho (*VD*): **Henry Beaulieu**
Boldieu, Scotty (*DS*): **Henry Beaulieu**
Boncoeur, Remi (*OR*): **Henry Cru**
Bromberg, Austen (*S*): **Alan Ansen**
Browning, Robert (*BS*): **William Morris**
Buchanan, Rosie (*DB*): **Natalie Jackson**
Buckle, Ed (*BD*): **Al Hinkle**
Buckle, Helen (*VC*): **Helen Hinkle**
Buckle, Slim (*VC*): **Al Hinkle**
Buferd, Biff (*VC*): **Bob Burford**
Buferd, Vera (*BD*): **Beverley Burford**
Byers, Burnie (*DB*): **Blackie Burns**
Cacoethes, Reinhold (*DB*): **Kenneth Rexroth**
Camille (*OR*): **Carolyn Cassady**
Carmody, Frank (*S*): **William S. Burroughs**
Cassidy, Maggie (*MC, VD*): **Mary Carney**
Cecily (*VD*): **Céline Young**
Chapman, Jay (*VC*): **Jay Landesman**
Clancy, Timmy (*MC, BD, VD*): **Jim O'Dea**
Cole, Pauline Moe (*MC, VD*): **Margaret Coffey**
Comucca, Ricci (*S*): **Richie Komuca**
Cordavan, Paddy (*S*): **Peter van Meter**

Coughlin, Warren (*DB*): **Philip Whalen**
D'Angeli, David (*DA*): **Philip Lamantia**
Da Pavia, Francis (*DB*): **Philip Lamantia**
Dabney, Billie (*BS*): **Jackie Gibson Mercer**
Dabney, Elliot (*BS*): **Eric Gibson**
Damion (*OR*): **Lucien Carr**
Damlette, Al/Mal (*DA, BS, T, BD*): **Al Sublette**
Darkovsky, Simon (*DA, BD*): **Peter Orlovsky**
de Maubris, Claude (*VD*): **Lucien Carr**
Dennison, Mary (*TC*): **Joan Vollmer Adams**
Dennison, Will (*TC; H*): **William S. Burroughs**
Derounian, Chuck (*VD*): **George Avakian**
di Chili, Richard (*DA*): **Peter du Peru**
Diane (*VC*): **Diana Hansen**
Diefendorf, Bud (*DB*): **Claude Dahlenburg**
Doll, Denver D. (*OR*) **Justin W. Brierly**
Donald, Geoffrey (*DA*): **Robert Duncan**
Donnelly, Rob (*DA*): **Bob Donlin**
Dorie (*OR*): **Vicki Russell**
Duluoz Gerard (*VG, DS*): **Gerard Kerouac**
Duluoz, Emil (*VG, VD, MC, DS*): **Leo Alcide Kerouac**
Duluoz, Jack (*VC, DS, MC, VG, T, DA, BS, SP, VD*): **Jack Kerouac**
Dunkel, Ed (*OR*): **Al Hinkle**
Dunkel, Galatea (*OR*): **Helen Hinkle**
Edna (*BD, VD*): **Edie Parker**
Elgins, Kyles (*VD*): **Kells Elvins**
Elly (*VC*): **Edie Parker**
Erickson, Ruth (*DA*): **Helen Elliot**
Evans, June (*BD, DA, VD*): **Jane Vollmer Adams**
Evelyn (*VC*): **Carolyn Cassady**
Fagan, Ben (*BS*): **Philip Whalen**
Fairbrother, Alex (*DB*): **John Montgomery**
Finistra (*VC, BD*): **William Cannastra**
Fitzpatrick, Bennet (*S*): **Whit Burnett**
Fitzpatrick, Walt (*S*): **David Burnett**
Fournier, Ed (*OR*): **Ed Sousiox**
Fox, Mardou (*S*): **Alene Lee**
Gaines, Old Bull (*DA, T, BD*): **Bill Garver**
Garden, Harry (*DA*): **Louis Ginsberg**
Garden, Irwin (*VD, DA, BS, VC, BD*): **Allen Ginsberg**
George (*DB*): **Peter Orlovsky**
Gilhooley, Mary (*TC*): **Mary Carney**
Gligoric, Yuri (*S*): **Gregory Corso**
Goldbrook, Alvah (*DB*): **Allen Ginsberg**
Gray, Ed (*VC*): **Ed White**
Gray, Tim (*OR*): **Ed White**
Greb, Rollo (*OR*): **Alan Ansen**
Green, Guy/Al (*BD*): **Ed White**
Gringas, Bruno (*DS*): **Duke Chiungas**

Gringas, Duke (*VC*): **Duke Chiungas**
Gringas, Telemachus (*VD*): **Duke Chiungas**
Hampshire, Dicky (*TC, DS, VD*) **Billy Chandler**
Harper (*VC*): **Bill Garver**
Hassel, Elmer (*OR*): **Herbert Huncke**
Hayes, Val (*VC*): **Hal Chase**
Heaper, Ruth (*DA*): **Helen Weaver**
Hindenberg, Bob (*VC, BD*): **Bob Brandenberg**
Hingham, Hal (*OR*): **Alan Harrington**
Hubbard, Bull (*VC, DS, DA, BD*): **William S. Burroughs**
Hubbard, June (*VC*): **Joan Vollmer Adams**
Hubbard, Will Holmes (*VD*): **William S. Burroughs**
Huck (*VC, BD*): **Herbert Huncke**
Inez (*OR*): **Diana Hansen**
James, Stephanie (*VC*): **Stephanie Stewart**
Jane (*S, OR*): **Joan Vollmer Adams**
Janie (*H*): **Edie Parker**
Joanna (*VC*): **LuAnne Henderson**
Johnson, Dorothy (*OR*): **Helen Tomson**
Johnson, Earl (*VC*): **Bill Tomson**
Johnson, Helen (*VC*): **Helen Tomson**
Johnson, Roy (*OR*): **Bill Tomson**
Josephine (*VC, DA, BD*): **Dusty Moreland**
Julien (*DA*): **Lucien Carr**
Junkey (*TC*): **Herbert Huncke**
Kazarakis, Johnnny (*MC, VD*): **Johnny Koumentzalis**
King, Chad (*OR*): **Hal Chase**
King, Val (*VC*): **Hal Chase**
Laura (*OR*): **Joan Haverty**
Laurier, Ed (*VC*): **Ed Sousiox**
Lauzon, Albert (Lousy) (*MC, DS*): **Roland Salvas**
Lavalina, Arail (*S*): **Gore Vidal**
Lee, Dodie (*OR*): **Julie Burroughs**
Lee, Old Bull (*OR*): **William S. Burroughs**
Lee, Ray (*OR*): **William Burroughs Jr.**
Leroy (*S*): **Neal Cassady**
Levesque, Guy (*DA*): **Robert LaVigne**
Levinsky, Leon (*TC*): **Allen Ginsberg**
Libble, Lou (*MC, VD*): **Lou Little**
Lipp, Barbara (*DA*): **Elise Cowen**
Lisle, Shelley (*BD*): **Stanley Gould**
Love, Julien (*VC; BD*): **Lucien Carr**
Love, Nessa (*VC*): **Cessa Carr**
Low, Charley (*VC, BD*): **Charlie Mew**
Low, Jimmy (*DA, VC*): **Charlie Mew**
Lucille (*OTR*): **Pauline**
Luke, Big (*DB*): **Paul Blake**
Luke, Little (*DB*): **Paul Blake Jr.**
Ma, Arthur (*BS*): **Victor Wong**

MacArthur, Ian (*OR*): **John Clellon Holmes**
MacJones, Balliol (*S*): **John Clellon Holmes**
Macy, John (*VC*): **John Kingsland**
Macy, Ronald (*BD*): **John Kingsland**
Major, Roland (*OR*): **Allan Temko**
Mannerly, Justin G. (*VC*): **Justin W. Brierly**
Mannerly, Manley (*BD*) **Justin W. Brierly**
Marker, Harvey (*DA*): **Norman Mailer**
Martin, George (*TC*): **Leo Alcide Kerouac**
Martin, Julian (*TC*): **Gerard Kerouac**
Martin, Margaret Courbet (*TC*): **Gabrielle L'Evesque Kerouac**
Martin, Peter (*TC*): **Jack Kerouac**
Marx, Carlo (*OR*): **Allen Ginsberg**
Mary Lou (*OR*): **LuAnne Henderson**
May, Irene (*BD*): **Alene Lee**
McCarthy (*VC*): **Jack Fitzgerald**
McClear, Patrick (*DA, BS*): **Michael McClure**
McLoch, Kevin (*DA*): **Locke McCorkle**
Meister, Waldo (*TC*): **David Kammerer**
Minko, Allen (*VC*): **Allan Temko**
Minko, Irving (*BD*): **Allan Temko**
Monahan, Sean (*DB*): **Locke McCorkle**
Monsanto, Lorenzo (*BS*): **Lawrence Ferlinghetti**
Moorad, Adam (*S*): **Allen Ginsberg**
Moore, Brue (*DA*): **Brew Moore**
Moriarty, Amy (*OR*): **Cathy Cassady**
Moriarty, Dean (*OR*): **Neal Cassady**
Moriarty, Joanie (*OR*): **Jamie Cassady**
Morley, Henry (*DB*): **John Montgomery**
Mulverhill, Danny (D. J.) (*TC*): **George Apostolos**
Nardine (*VC*): **Mardean**
Newman, Alyce (*DA*): **Joyce Glassman**
Nicholas, Fritz (*S*): **Bill Keck**
Nin (*DS, DB, MC*): **Caroline Kerouac**
O'Hara, Larry (*S*): **Jerry Newman**
O'Shay, Ike (*DB*): **Michael McClure**
Ogilvie, June (*BD*): **Joan Haverty**
Palmer, Edna (Johnnie) (*VD*): **Edie Parker**
Panos, Alex (*TC*): **Sammy Sampas**
Paradise, Sal (*OR*): **Jack Kerouac**
Paul (*DA*): **Claude Dahlenburg**
Percepied, Leo (*S*): **Jack Kerouac**
Pomeray, Cody (*VC, DB, DA, BS*): **Neal Cassady**
Pomeray, Diana (*VC*): **Diana Hansen**
Pomeray, Emily (*VC*): **Cathy Cassady**
Pomeray, Gaby (*VC*): **Jamie Cassady**
Pomeray, Timmy (*VC*): **John Allen Cassady**
Pomeray, Timmy John (*BS*): **John Allen Cassady**
Randall, Merrill (*DA*): **Robert Merrill**

Random, Varnum (*DA*): **Randall Jarrell**
Rappaport, Carl (*VC*): **Carl Solomon**
Rawlins, Babe (*OR*): **Beverley Burford**
Rawlins, Ray (*OR*): **Bob Burford**
Richman, Danny (*VC, BD*): **Jerry Newman**
Rigolopoulos, (*VD*): **George Apostolos**
Rigopoulos, G. J. (*DS, MC*): **George Apostolos**
Rose, Gerard (*BD*): **Rosenberg, Anton**
Rosemarie (*DA, BS, BD*): **Natalie Jackson**
Rosenberg, Joey (*BS*): **Jarry Heiserberg**
Rouleau, Scotcho (*TC*): **Henry Beaulieu**
Roxanne (*S*): **Iris Brodie**
Ryder, Japhy (*DB*): **Gary Snyder**
Ryder, Rhoda (*DB*): **Thea Snyder**
Ryko, Mike (*H*): **Jack Kerouac**
Sand, Harold (*S*): **William Gaddis**
Santos, James G. (*MC*): **Charles Sampas**
Savakis, Sabby (*VD*): **Sammy Sampas**
Savakis, Stavroula (*VD*): **Stella Sampas**
Savas (*VG*) **Sammy Sampas**
Saybrook, Tom (*OR*): **Ed Stringham**
Sebastian (*VC*): **Sammy Sampas**
Shephard, Stan (*OR*): **Frank Jeffries**
Sherman, Dave (*VC, BD*): **Frank Jeffries**
Smart, Lionel (*VC, MC, BD, VD*): **Seymour Wyse**
Smith, Judie (*TC*): **Edie Parker**
Smith, Ray (*DB*): **Jack Kerouac**
Snark, Tom (*OR*): **Jim Holmes**
St Clair, White (*MC*): **Red St Louis**
Steen, Jack (*S*): **Mason Hoffenberg**
Strange, Freddy (*VC*): **Freddy Strong**
Strauss, Sylvester (*S*): **David Diamond**
Stroheim, Dave (*VC*): **David Kammerer**
Swartz, Ramona (*BS*): **Lenore Kandel**
Swenson, Irwin (*VC, BD*): **Alan Ansen**
Terry (*OR*): **Bea Franco**
Tourian, Phillip (*H*): **Lucien Carr**
Tristessa (*T*): **Esperanza Villanueva**
Urso, Raphael (*DB, DA, BD*): **Gregory Corso**
Valencia, Gia (*DA*): **Gui de Angulo**
van Buder, Buddy (*VC, BD*): **Peter van Meter**
Vauriselle, Zaza (*MC*): **Jean Fourchette**
Vedder, Sam (*S*): **Lucien Carr**
Vicki (*VC*): **Vicki Russell**
Wagner, Jarry (*DA*): **Gary Snyder**
Wain, Dave (*BS*): **Lew Welch**
Wall, Ed (*OR*): **Don Uhl**
Wallenstein, Ross (*S*): **Stanley Gould**
Wallington, Early (*BD*): **Alan Harrington**

Watson, John (*VC*): **John Clellon Holmes**
Wehle, Ed (*VC*): **Don Uhl**
Whane, Arthur (*BS*): **Alan Watts**
"Wifey" (*VD*): **Stella Sampas**
Williams, Dr. (*DA*): **William Carlos Williams**
Winchel, Jimmy (*VD*): **Eddie Gilbert**
Wise Lazuli, Rose (*DA*): **Ruth Witt-Diamant**
Wohlstetter, Arlene (*S*): **Dusty Moreland**
Wood, Kenny (*TC*): **Lucien Carr**
Yturbide, Perry (*BS*): **James Perpignan**
Zagg, Little (*VC*): **Jack Melodias**
Zaza, Ali (*DS*): **Jean Fourchette**
Zouzou (*TC*): **Jean Fourchette**

Appendix B: Kerouac's Novels' Chronology and the Duluoz Saga

What follows are two alternative orderings of Kerouac's fiction. The first is an attempt to define the chronological order in which Kerouac worked on his fiction. This is followed by the novels' arrangement as a sequential saga about the Duluoz family and the life of Jack Duluoz.

One of my arguments is that the best approach to Kerouac's writings is to concentrate on the early writing first. If the novels are instead read as an unfolding saga, then two of his less well constructed works (the 'apprentice' *Town and the City* and the rambling *Vanity of Duluoz*) would be two of the first books to be read, while his better work would be encountered quite late on. A better starting-point is *On the Road*—and, arguably, the 1951 scroll version of *On the Road* is the one to read first.

B.i. Chronology

Arriving at a definitive chronological order to Kerouac's writing is not possible. Kerouac did not work sequentially on his books, not least because of the problems he experienced in getting his work published and the protracted negotiations he had with publishers. Instead he often worked on several projects at the same time, switching between them. In the list which follows, dates of composition appear beside the novels' titles, showing how such compositional overlapping occurs. The main period(s) of composition are indicated by bold type, and the date of actual publication by italics. The list is ordered on the basis of the date[s] when the majority of the writing was done This table includes the abbreviations for Kerouac's works used in the text:

The Town and the City	*TC*	**1945-1949**; 1950
And the Hippos Were Boiled in Their Tanks	*H*	**1945**; *2008*
On the Road	*OR*	1948-**1951-1957**; *1957*
Doctor Sax	*DS*	**1948-1952**; *1959*
Visions of Cody	*VC*	**1950-1952**; 1959 (excerpts); *1972*
Maggie Cassidy	*MC*	**1952-1953**; 1959
'The Railroad Earth'	'RE'	**1952-1953**; *1957*; *1960*
The Subterraneans	*S*	**1953**; *1958*
Book of Dreams	*BD*	1952-**1954-1960**; *1961*
'cityCityCITY	'CC'	**1954-1955**; *1959*
Mexico City Blues	*MB*	**1955**; 1956; *1959*
Visions of Gerard	*VG*	**1955-1956**; 1962; *1963*
Tristessa	*T*	**1955-1956**; *1960*
Old Angel Midnight	*OM*	**1956**; **1959**; *1959* (prts 1-49); *1961* (prts 50-51); *1964* (prts 50-67); *1993*
Dharma Bums	*DB*	**1957-1958**; *1958*
Desolation Angels	*DA*	**1956-1961**-1965; 1965

Big Sur	*BS*	**1961**; *1962*
Satori in Paris	*SP*	**1965**; 1966
Vanity of Duluoz	*VD*	[1941?-1945] **1962-1967**; *1968*
Pic	*P*	[1940] [1948] [1950] [1951] **1968**; *1971*

B.ii. The Duluoz Saga

If Kerouac's novels were to be arranged into a saga, outlining the history of the Duluoz family and Jack Duluoz in particular—something Kerouac maintained that he held as an objective—then the following order might be arrived at. It is important to note that there are some substantial overlaps, especially between his relatively early works, *The Town and the City*, *Visions of Gerard*, and *Doctor Sax*, and his last full-length novel, *Vanity of Duluoz*, which serves as a kind of 'patch-up' work, filling in the gaps left by his early writings. All these overlaps are indicated, except where they are very minor.

Visions of Gerard }
Doctor Sax }
The Town and the City }
Vanity of Duluoz } })
Maggie Cassidy } :
And the Hippos Were Boiled in Their Tanks)
Visions of Cody }
On the Road }
'The Railroad Earth'
The Subterraneans
Tristessa
Dharma Bums
Desolation Angels
Big Sur
Satori in Paris

Footnotes

Introduction

1. Kerouac, *Big Sur—BS.* References to Kerouac's writing appear with initials identifying the books. See Appendix B.i for the key. Plainly, any attempt to try to contain all this in a short introductory biography is doomed to fail. But I have tried my best. I need to thank those who have helped or supported me: in particular, Dave Moore, also Mary Dawson, Manju Jaidka and Ann Hurford—and, first and foremost, Maggie Ellis. Thanks also to Susan Forsyth for her copy-editing—(susan.forsyth@btinternet.com) This biography owes deep debts to Barry Gifford and Lawrence Lee, Gerald Nicosia and Ellis Amburn. Any errors, of course, remain my own responsibility.
2. Jack Kerouac, 'Essentials of Spontaneous Prose', 1959, rpt in *Good Blonde and Others*, San Francisco: Grey Fox Press, p.70.
3. Gerald Nicosia, *Memory Babe*, 1983; rpt. Harmondsworth: Penguin, 1986, p.39; Lucien Carr, quoted in Gifford and Lee, *Jack's Book: Jack Kerouac in the Lives and Words of His Friends*, London: Hamish Hamilton, 1979, p.46; Glassman, quoted in Gifford and Lee, p.236.
4. Jack Kerouac, 'Essentials', p.70.
5. Malcolm Cowley, quoted in Gifford and Lee, p.206.
6. Jack Kerouac, 'Essentials of Spontaneous Prose', p.70.
7. Kerouac, 'Essentials', p.70.
8. John Clellon Holmes, quoted in Gifford and Lee, pp. 156-57.
9. Kerouac, 'Essentials', p.70.
10. John Clellon Holmes, Letter to Joy Walsh, 1972, rpt. in *Remembering Jack Kerouac*, Coventry: The Beat Scene Press, 2008, n.p. [p.30].

Jack Kerouac—Outside Writing

1. Jack Kerouac, in Remi Férland, ed., 'Jack Kérouac au/on *Sel de la Semaine* (Radio-Canada, Montreal, 1967), *Les Avant-Dire de la Rencontre Internationale Jack Kérouac*, Quebec: Le Secrétariat permanent des peuples francophones, Septembre, 1987, p.19. The phrase is translated by Paul Fortin and Eric Waddell from the joual: 'ch'sais faire ... écrire des histoires, pis c'est toutte' (p.10).
2. See Paul Maher, Jr., *Kerouac: The Definitive Biography*, London: Taylor Trade Publishing, 2004, pp. 3ff. As Tom Clark points out, in the last decade of his life, Kerouac's claims became ever more inflated: Clark, *Jack Kerouac*, p.4.
3. Nicosia, *Memory Babe*, p.22.
4. Clark, p.5.
5. Holmes, 2008, p.3.
6. Nicosia, p.2.
7. Nicosia, p.23. For an account of Kerouac's early years in Lowell, see Roger J. Brunelle, 'Les premières années de l'enfance de Jack

Kérouac', in Pierre Anctil, et. al, eds., *Un Homme Grand: Jack Kerouac at the Crossroads of Many Cultures*, Ottawa: Carleton, 1990, pp.125-144.

8. Charles Jarvis, quoted in Gifford and Lee, *Jack's Book*, p.217.
9. Dave Moore points out that Jim Perrizo discovered that Nicosia was wrong to rely on Parker's claim that Kerouac met her before 1942. Moore, letter to R. J. Ellis, 27 February 1998.
10. Charles E. Jarvis, *Visions of Kerouac: The Life of Jack Kerouac*, New York: Ithaca Press, 1974, p.9.
11. Baudelaire, 'Le Voyage', *Les Fleurs du Mal*, 1861, rpt. *Les Fleurs du Mal et autres poëmes*, Paris: La Renaissance du Livre, 1921, p.152.
12. Kerouac, diary entry for Nov. 16, 1944, quoted in Charters, ed., *Letters* I, p.81; Nicosia, p.134. For a discussion of the significance of Alfred Korzybski on the Beats, see David Ingram, 'William Burroughs and Language', in A. Robert Lee, ed., *The Beat Generation Writers*, pp.95-97 and passim. Dave Moore alerted me to the fact that, though Kerouac first encountered Spengler when still in Lowell, he probably did not read him until Burroughs gave him a copy. Moore, letter to R. J. Ellis, 27 February 1998.
13. Rosalind Rosenberg, *Divided Lives: American Women in the Twentieth Century*, New York: Hill and Wang, 1992, p.152.
14. Joan Haverty Kerouac, *Nobody's Wife: The Smart Alec and the King of the Beats*, Berkeley: Creative Arts Books, 2000, p.176.
15. Neal Cassady, 'Letter from Neal Cassady to Jack Kerouac', 7 March 1947, *Collected Letters, 1944-1967*, ed. Dave Moore London: Penguin, pp. 17-18. See also Neal Cassady, *The First Third*, San Francisco: City Lights, 1971, pp.124-126 (125). See also Nicosia, p.183.
16. Haverty Kerouac, p.177.
17. Lucien Carr, quoted in Gifford and Lee, p.46.
18. 'Letter from Neal Cassady to Jack Kerouac', 7 January 1948, rpt. in Neal Cassady, *Collected Letters*, p. 69; 'Letter from Neal Cassady to Jack Kerouac', 7 March 1947, rpt. in Cassady, *Collected Letters* I, p.19.
19. Nicosia, p.233.
20. John Clellon Holmes, 'The Name of the Game', *Nothing More to Declare*, London: Andre Deutsch, pp.106-107.
21. Kerouac, quoted in Nicosia, p.253.
22. John Clellon Holmes, quoted in Christopher Lehmann-Haupt, 'Books of the Times', *The New York Times* Arts Section 14 January 1983: 23.
23. Kerouac, quoted in Nicosia, pp.263, 265.
24. Kerouac, 'Journal during first stages of "On the Road"', 25 March 1949, quoted in Nicosia, p.265.
25. Kerouac, quoted in Nicosia, p.308
26. Nicosia, p.269.
27. Kerouac, quoted in Nicosia, p.279.
28. Kerouac, quoted in Nicosia, p.295.

29. Nicosia quotes Cassady: '"its watermelon time again"', p.323.
30. Kerouac, quoted in Nicosia, p.324.
31. Kerouac, quoted in Nicosia, p.327.
32. 'Letter to Neal Cassady', 6 October 1950, Charters, ed., *Selected Letters* I, p.233.
33. Cassady, *Collected Letters*, pp.244-255. Only 5,100 words survive; Nicosia, pp.335-336; Joan Kerouac Haverty, quoted in Charters, ed. *Selected Letters* I, p.233.
34. Kerouac, quoted in Clark, p.95.
35. 'Letter to Neal Cassady', 27 December 1950, Charters, ed., *Selected Letters* I, p.242.
36. See, e.g., Kerouac's letters to Cassady of 28 December 1950 and 3 January 1951, in Charters, ed., *Selected Letters* I, pp.246-273.
37. Neal Cassady, 'Letter to Jack Kerouac', Dec. 30, 1950, quoted in Charters, *Kerouac: A Biography*, San Francisco: Straight Arrow Press, p.123.
38. Cassady, *The First Third*, pp.81-82.
39. Carolyn Cassady, commentary in Neal Cassady, *The First Third and Other Writings*, Expanded Edition, San Francisco: City Lights, 1981, p.140.
40. Ted Berrigan, *Paris Review* interview with Kerouac, No.43 Summer 1968, rpt. in Scott Donaldson, ed., *On the Road: Text and Criticism*, New York: Penguin Books, 1979, pp.538-572, p.541.
41. Lucien Carr, quoted in Cook, p.74. Kerouac, in 'The Origins of the Beat Generation', reports that he typed out the roll in May, not April, Playboy Vol. 6 No. 6, June 1959, p.42. This discrepancy is unlikely to be reconciled. See also Gussow, 'Bohemia Revisited', pp.291-311. Dave Moore points out that it is a common myth that the scroll included no commas and few periods. His position was, rightly, that the 1957 (published) version does not contain 'major differences in ... punctuation' ('The Scroll Revealed', The Kerouac Connection, No. 17, Spring 1989). However, the publication of the scroll version in 2007 now allows close comparison, which shows many, sometimes highly significant changes. It needs to be added that the 2007 published version of the scroll unfortunately contains many mis-transcriptions.

    Scroll (1951): '... he had to sweat to and curse to make a living and so on. My first impression of Neal was of a young Gene Autry— trim, thin-hipped, blue eyes, with a real Oklahoma accent. In fact he'd just been working on a ranch'.

    Book (1957): '... he had to sweat and curse to make a living and so on. You saw that in the way he stood bobbing his head, always looking down, nodding, like a young boxer to instructions, throwing in a thousand 'Yeses' and 'That's rights'. My first impression of Dean was of a young Gene Autry—trim, thin-hipped, blue-eyed, with a real Oklahoma accent—a side-

> burned hero of the snowy West. In fact he'd just been working on a ranch' (OR, 6).

In these differences I believe a slightly greater instability can be seen in the later version. Dean is now more plainly represented as a site of conflicts in Sal's portrait: like a young boxer, on the one hand—slightly excessive in his desire to please and slightly too fired-up, whilst, on the other, mythologized, less reliably, as a 'hero of the snowy West', in line with Sal's greater tendency to romanticize in the 1957 version (see Chapter Three). Such changes make it clear why Cowley described Kerouac as 'good [at] revision' (Gifford and Lee, *Jack's Book*, p.206). I have taken the scroll transcript from Dave Moore, 'ON THE ROAD: From the Scroll Typescript by Jack Kerouac', *The Kerouac Connection*, No. 10, April 1986. The 2007 published version unfortunately contains many mis-transcriptions.

42. See Jerome Beatty, 'Trade Winds', in *The Saturday Review*, 28 September 1957, reprinted in Paul Maher, Jr., *Empty Phantoms: Interviews and Encounters with Jack Kerouac*, New York: Thunder's Mouth Press, 2005: p.51; Haverty Kerouac, 2000: p.202.
43 Allen Ginsberg, [Review of *Dharma Bums*], *Village Voice* 12 November 1958, pp. 3-5.
44. 'Letter to Hal Chase', Oct. 19, 1948, Charters, ed., *Selected Letters of Jack Kerouac* I, p.170.
45. Lucien Carr, quoted in McNally, p.67.
46. John Montgomery, 'Jack Kerouac and the San Francisco Renaissance', 1974, unpublished typescript, Birmingham University Library, p.26.
47. Jack Kerouac, *Selected Letters*, Vol.1, p.423. My thanks to Dave Moore for pointing this out.
48. Ginsberg, [Review of *Dharma Bums*], p.5.
49. Kerouac, 'Letter to Allen Ginsberg', 18 May 1952, Charters, ed., *Selected Letters* I, p.356.
50. Ibid., p.355.
51. Nicosia, p.367.
52. Kerouac, quoted in Hunt, *Kerouac's Crooked Road*, p.147.
53. Carolyn Cassady explains that she was never quite sure whether by 'fellaheen' Kerouac meant 'the essence of a culture ... or, as Spengler used it (where Jack got the term) ... the "residue" of a culture after it has collapsed', quoted in Charters, ed., *Selected Letters*, p.347.
54. *Doctor Sax*'s weaving together of dream and reality draws on Kerouac's experiences of living with Burroughs whilst working on this text, see Clark, *Jack Kerouac*, p.110. In particular, Burroughs' use of 'facts on many levels'—realistic, but also fantastic, surrealist—in his Factualist style (as he called it) bears upon the construction of *Doctor Sax*. Quite possibly, however, this was not simply a one-way process, as Kerouac and Burroughs exchanged ideas. Certainly, Kerouac's writing in *Sax* remains different from

Burroughs', in that it reads as 'more poetry than prose', Jack Kerouac, [Journal extract], Friday March 25, 1949, quoted in Moore, 'Extracts from Kerouac's "On the Road" Journal', p.6.
55. Kerouac, 'Letter to John Clellon Holmes', June 5, 1952, Charters, ed., *Selected Letters*, p.371; see also Hunt, p.147.
56. Holmes, 2008, p.12.
57. For a discussion of Kerouac's debts to *The Shadow* and other comic books, see Steve Turner, *Angelheaded Hipster*, p.37.
58. The masturbation passages can be found in James Joyce, *Ulysses*, 1922, rpt. Harmondsworth: Penguin, 1992, pp.365-67, 703-74. A large section of *Ulysses* is laid out as dramatic dialogue: see pp.425-532. Pages 380-425 of *Ulysses* are written in a series of different literary and demotic registers—again, a source of inspiration for *Visions of Cody*.
59. Nicosia notes this omnipresence of time and death in *Memory Babe*, p.4. Tytell discusses the clash between Lowell domesticity and New York's allure in *Naked Angels*, p.191
60. Kerouac, Letter to Ed White, 1953, quoted in Nicosia, p.446.
61. Kerouac, quoted in Nicosia, p.442.
62. Jack Kerouac, in his 'Written Address to the Italian Judge', *Evergreen Review* Vol. 7 No. 31, 1963, p.109, notes how *The Subterraneans'* confessional form owes a strong debt to Dostoyevsky's *Notes from the Underground*.
63. Leroi Jones (Amiri Baraka), 'Letter to the Editors', *Evergreen Review* Vol. 2 No. 8 (Spring 1959), pp.254-5.
64. Nicosia, p.460.
65. Stendhal, *The Red and the Black*, 1830, rpt. Harmondsworth: Penguin, 1953.
66. William Carlos Williams, 'This is just to say', in William Carlos Williams, *The Collected Early Poems*, London: MacGibbon and Key, 1951, p.354.
67. See also the 83rd chorus of *Mexico City Blues*, which openly refers to Williams' 'Poem', 'As the cat', Williams, *Collected Early Poems*, p.340.
68. Kerouac, 'Essentials', p.72.
69. '6 Poets at 6 Gallery' was how it appeared on the invitation; see Turner, p.153.
70. McClure, 'Introduction' to *Old Angel Midnight*, xv.
71. See Anthony Linick, 'A History of the American Literary Avant-Garde', Ph.D. dissertation, University of California, Los Angeles, 1965, pp.41ff.; Lawrence Ferlinghetti uses the term 'carpetbaggers', in Turner, p.163.
72. Gary Snyder, quoted in Nicosia, p.495.
73. See Beaulieu, *Jack Kerouac*, p.23, for an account of the polluted condition of 1920s' and 1930s' Lowell.
74. See Moore, 2004: passim.
75. Kerouac, quoted in Clark, p.153.
76. The first part, 'October in the Railroad Earth' appeared in *Evergreen Review* Vol. 1 No. 2, Summer 1957, pp.119-36. The

remainder, 'Conclusion of the Railroad Earth', appeared in *Evergreen Review* Vol. 4 No. 11, Jan-Feb 1960, pp.37-59. I have chosen to refer to these for my quotations. 'The Railroad Earth' appears as the second story in the collection, *Lonesome Traveler* (New York: McGraw-Hill, 1960).

77. Kerouac, quoted in Clark, p.161.
78. Jack Kerouac, to Neal Cassady, 26 October 1957, quoted in Clark, p.165.
79. Truman Capote, quoted in Nicosia, p.588. It can be argued that this intended insult is in fact a type of compliment, recognizing how Kerouac had moved writing on from pen and ink into the age of the typewriter, by using it—at breakneck speed—to compose his fiction and poetry.
80. See Tytell, *Naked Angels*, pp.25-27, 74-77, and Jones, *Map of Mexico City Blues*, Chapter 6.
81. Hipkiss gives an extended account of Kerouac's variety of Mahayana Buddhism, *Jack Kerouac: Prophet*, pp.63ff. See also Jones, Chapter 6. In this, Jones describes the Buddhism in *the Dharma Bums* as 'often ... preach, even sappy', p.106. Ralph Lombreglia and Kate Bernhardt's *A Jack Kerouac ROMnibus* (Chapel Hill and New York: Penguin Books and Black Mountain Multimedia, 1995) gives the best account of the book's Buddhism.
82. See Jones, p.110 and passim and Carl T. Jackson, 'The counterculture looks East: beat writers and Asian religion', *American Studies*, Vol. 29, Spring 1988, pp.51-70.
83. See Davidson, *The San Francisco Renaissance*; see also Linick, 'A History of the American Literary Avant-Garde', pp.56ff.
84. Lawrence Ferlinghetti, quoted in Nicosia, p.564.
85. Holmes, 2007, p.8.
86. 'Letter to John Clellon Holmes', May 27, 1956, Charters, ed., *Selected Letters*, p.580.
87. Nicosia, *Memory Babe*, p.517.
88. Nicosia suggests the book be read as 'a confessional dialogue between the writer and his accusers ... the chief inquisitorial voice belonging to Lucien Carr', p.517.
89. See Clark Coolidge, 'Kerouac', p.45.
90. The phrase was probably coined by Herb Caen in a column, 'Pocketful of Notes' in the *San Francsisco Chronicle*, 2 April 1958. An alternative explanation is that Bob Kaufman first used it orally in one his improvised poems on some earlier occasion. See Jay Parini, ed., *The Oxford Encyclopedia of American Literature*, Oxford: Oxford University Press, 2004, p.143.
91. We know that Kerouac regarded *Big Sur* as 'honester' than his other books. See Nicosia, *Memory Babe*, p.629.
92. Kerouac described the novel as written with the 'raciness and freedom and humor of jazz', 'Letter to Sterling Lord', 7 October 1956, in Charters, ed., Selected Letters I, p.588.
93. I am partly indebted to French, *Jack Kerouac*, p.94, for this point.

94. See Takashi Ikemoto's definition in Stryk and Ikemoto, eds., *The Penguin Book of Zen Poetry*, p.36.
95. Tytell, *Naked Angels*, p.208.
96. See Nicosia, *Memory Babe*, pp.659-60.
97. This is a translation of the original words: 'il oscille entre la panique at la colère et ...il était allé chercher querelle dans quelque taverne', Fernard Séguin, quoted in Remi Férland, ed., 'Jack Kerouac au/on *Sel de la Semaine'*, p. 21.
98. Dick McBride, 'Shouting Down the Line', *The Beat Journal*, Vol. 1 (1995), pp.86-90. See also transcript of interview with Dick McBride by R. J. Ellis and Mary Dawson, Nov. 7, 1996, Dick McBride papers, The Nottingham Trent University Library.
99. See Hunt, *Kerouac's Crooked Road*, pp.102-4.

Bibliography

Primary References

The following list includes all the work of Kerouac to which I have referred; the editions that I have used for my abbreviated page references are emboldened. This is not an exhaustive bibliography.

'Aftermath: The Philosophy of the Beat Generation', *Esquire*, Vol. 49 No. 3, March 1958, pp.24, 26.

'After Me, the Deluge', *Chicago Tribune* Sunday Magazine section, September 28, 1969, pp.20-23.

'Among the Iroquois', *City Lights Journal*, Vol. 1, 1963, pp.43-45.

And the Hippos Were Boiled in Their Tanks, New York: Grove Press, 2008.

Atop an Underwood, ed. Paul Marion, New York: Viking Penguin, 1999.

Beat Generation: 3-Act Play, 1957; rpt. Thunder's Mouth Press, New York: 2005.

'Belief and Technique for Modern Prose', *Evergreen Review* Vol. 2 No. 8, Spring 1959, p.57.

***Big Sur*, New York: Farrar, Straus and Cudahy, 1962.**

Book of Blues, New York: Penguin, 1995. Introduction by Robert Creeley.

Book of Dreams, San Francisco: City Lights, 1961.

Book of Haikus, ed. Regina Weinreich, New York: Penguin Poets, 2003.

'CITYCitycity', Leroi Jones, ed., *The Moderns*, New York: Corinth Books, 1963, pp.250-265.

'Conclusion of the Railroad Earth', *Evergreen Review* Vol. 4 No. 11, Jan.-Feb. 1960, pp.37-59.

Dear Carolyn: Letters to Carolyn Cassady, California PA: the unspeakable visions of the individual, 1983.

***Desolation Angels*, New York: Coward-McCann, 1965. Introduction by Seymour Krim.**

***Doctor Sax: Faust Part Three*, New York: Grove Press, 1959.**

'Essentials of Spontaneous Prose', *Evergreen Review*, Vol.2 No.5, Summer 1958, pp.72-73.

Excerpts from Visions of Cody, New York: New Directions, 1960.

'Extracts from Kerouac's "On the Road" Journal, November 1948-April 1949 and "On the Road" (2nd version), March 1949-June 1949', unpublished typescript, ed. Dave Moore, n.d., The Nottingham Trent University Library.

'Good Blonde', *Playboy*, January 1965, pp. 139-140, 192-194.

Good Blonde and Others, San Francisco: Grey Fox Press, rev. ed., 1994. Edited by Donald Allen. Preface by Robert Creeley. [includes 'cityCityCITY']

Heaven and Other Poems, Bolinas: Grey Fox Press, 1977.

Jack Kerouac—Windblown World: the Journals of Jack Kerouac 1947-1954, New York: Viking Penguin, 2004.

'Jazz of the Beat Generation', *New World Writing* 7 (April 1955).

'Lamb, No Lion', *Pageant*, February 1958, pp. 160-61.

'Letters from Jack Kerouac to Ed White', 1947-1968', *The Missouri Review*, Vol. 17 No. 3, 1994, pp. 107-160.

Lonesome Traveler, New York: McGraw-Hill, 1960.

***Maggie Cassidy*, New York: Avon Book Division, Hearst Corporation, 1959.**

Mexico City Blues, New York: Grove Press, 1959.

'October in the Railroad Earth', *Evergreen Review*, Vol. 1 No. 2, Summer 1957, pp. 119-136.

'Old Angel Midnight', *Big Table*, Vol. 1 No. 1, 1959, pp. 7-42.

'Old Angel Midnight Part Two', *Evergreen Review*, Vol. 8 No. 33, Aug.-Sept. 1964, pp.68-71, 91.

***Old Angel Midnight*, San Francisco: Grey Fox Press, 1993. Edited by Donald Allen. Prefaces by Ann Charters and Michael McClure.**

On the Road, New York: Viking Press, 1957.

On the Road [scroll version], New York: Penguin Viking, 2007.

'On the Road to Florida', *Evergreen Review*, Vol. 14 No. 74, January 1970, pp.43-47, 64.

'*On the Road*: From the Scroll Typescript', Dave Moore, ed., *The Kerouac Connection*, No. 10, April 1986, pp.7-8.

***Pic*, New York: Grove Press, 1966.**

'*Paris Review* interview', with Ted Berrigan et. al., *Paris Review*, No. 43, Summer 1968, pp.60-109.

Pomes All Sizes, San Francisco: City Lights Books, 1992. Introduction by Allen Ginsberg.

Pull My Daisy, New York: Grove Press, 1961. Text ad-libbed by Jack Kerouac for the film by Robert Frank and Alfred Leslie. Introduction by Jerry Tallmer.

Rimbaud, San Francisco: City Lights Books, 1960.

San Francisco Blues, New York: Penguin, 1995, pp.3-81.

'Satori in Paris: I' *Evergreen Review*, Vol. 10 No. 39, February 1966, pp.17-21, 74-79.

'Satori in Paris: II' *Evergreen Review*, Vol. 10 No. 40, April 1966, pp.56-59, 78-88.

'Satori in Paris: III' *Evergreen Review*, Vol. 10 No. 41, June 1966, pp.50-53, 80-90.

***Satori in Paris*, New York: Grove Press, 1966.**

Scattered Poems, San Francisco: City Lights Books, 1971.

Selected Letters of Jack Kerouac, vol. 1 *1940-1956*, vol. 2 *1957-1969*, Ann Charters, ed., London: Viking Penguin, 1995, 1999.

Some of the Dharma. New York: Viking Press, 1997.

'The Beginning of Bop', *Escapade*, April 1959, pp.4-5, 52.

Take Care of My Ghost, Ghost, [Jack Kerouac, Allen Ginsberg, co-authors], New York: Ghost Press, 1977.

'The Brothers', *Horace Mann Quarterly*, Fall 1939, pp.11-13.

***The Dharma Bums*, New York: Viking Press, 1958.**

'The Electrocution of Block 38383939383 ...', *Nugget*, August 1959, pp.12-14, 57-60. [rpt. as 'cityCityCITY' in *Good Blonde and Others*].

'The Great Western Bus Ride', *Esquire*, March 1970, pp.136-7, 158.
'The Murder of Swinburne', *Evergreen Review*, Vol. 12 No. 51, February 1968, pp.60-63, 110-118.
'The Origins of the Beat Generation', *Playboy* Vol. 6 No. 6, June 1959, pp. 31-32, 42, 79.
The Portable Jack Kerouac, Ann Charters, ed., New York: Viking, 1995.
The Scripture of the Golden Eternity, New York: Totem Press, 1960.
***The Subterraneans*, New York: Avon Publications, 1959. Preface by Henry Miller.**
***The Town and the City*, New York: Harcourt Brace, 1950.**
'Three Excerpts from "Visions of Cody"', Seymour Krim, ed., *The Beats*, Greenwich, Conn.: Fawcett Publications, 1960, pp. 34-43.
Trip Trap: Haiku Along the Road from San Francisco to New York 1959, [Jack Kerouac, Albert Saijo, Lew Welch, co-authors], Bolinas, Calif.: Grey Fox Press, 1973.
***Tristessa*, New York: Avon Book Division, Hearst Corporation, 1960.**
Two Early Stories New York: Aloes Editions, 1973. [Contains 'The Brothers' and 'Une Veille de Noël'].
Uncollected Writings, New York: 'C' Press, 1971.
'Une Veille de Noël', *Horace Mann Quarterly*, Summer 1940, pp.16-19.
***Vanity of Duluoz: An Adventurous Education, 1936-1946*, New York: Coward-McCann, 1968.**
***Visions of Cody*, New York: McGraw-Hill, 1972. Introduction by Allen Ginsberg.**
Visions of Gerard, New York: Farrar, Straus and Company, 1963.
Wake Up: A Life of the Buddha, New York: Viking, 2008.
'Written Address to the Italian Judge', *Evergreen Review* Vol. 7 No. 31, 1963, pp.108-110.

Secondary References

This pocket biography is particularly indebted to Dave Moore, Gerald Nicosia, Ellis Amburn, Barry Gifford and Lawrence Lee.

Anctil, Pierre et. al., eds. *Un Homme Grand: Jack Kerouac at the Crossroads of Many Cultures*, Ottawa: Carleton University Press, 1990.
Amburn, Ellis. Subterranean Kerouac: the Hidden Life of Jack Kerouac. New York: St Martin's Press, 1998.
Anctil, Pierre. 'Jack Kerouac and the Problem of Joual Aesthetics', Moody Street Irregulars, No. 11, 1982, pp.5-6.
Askew, Melvin W. 'Quests, Cars and Kerouac', University of Kansas City Review, Vol. 28 No. 3 (Spring, 1962), pp.231-240.
Bakhtin, Mikhail. *The Dialogic Imagination*, ed. Michael Holquist, trans. Caryl Emerson and Michael Holquist, Austin; University of Texas Press, 1981.
Baraka, Amiri. See Leroi Jones.

Baudelaire, Charles. *Les Fleurs du Mal*, 1861, rpt. *Les Fleurs de Mal et autres poëmes*, Paris: La Renaissance du Livre, 1921.
Beaulieu, Victor Levy. *Jack Kerouac: a chicken essay*, trans. Sheila Fischman, Toronto: Coach House Press, 1979.
Berrigan, Ted. Interview with Jack Kerouac, *Paris Review*, No. 43 Summer 1968, pp.60-109.
Brunelle, Roger J. 'Les premières années de l'enfance de Jack Kérouac', in Pierre Anctil, et. al, eds., *Un Homme Grand: Jack Kerouac at the Crossroads of Many Cultures*, Ottawa: Carleton, 1990, pp.125-144.
Caen, Herb Caen. 'Pocketful of Notes', *San Francisco Chronicle*, 2 April 1958.
Cassady, Carolyn. *Heart Beat: My Life with Jack & Neal*, Berkeley: Creative Arts, 1976.
Cassady, Carolyn. *Off the Road: Twenty Years with Cassady, Kerouac and Ginsberg*, London: Black Spring Press, 1990.
Cassady, Neal. *The First Third*, San Francisco: City Lights, 1971; revised ed., 1981.
Cassady, Neal. *Collected Letters, 1944-1967*, ed. Dave Moore London: Penguin, 2004.
Céline, Louis-Ferdinand. *Journey to the End of the Night*, 1932, rpt., trans. Ralph Manheim, London: John Calder, 1988.
Challis, Chris. *Quest for Kerouac*, London: Faber and Faber, 1984.
Charters, Ann. *Kerouac: A Biography*, San Francisco: Straight Arrow Press, 1973.
Charters, Ann. '"Letting Go" in Writing', in Jack Kerouac, *Old Angel Midnight*, San Francisco: Grey Fox Press, pp. ix-xii.
Charters, Ann. *Selected Letters of Jack Kerouac, 1940-1951*, London: Viking Penguin, 1995.
Charters, Ann. *Selected Letters*
Clark, Tom. *Jack Kerouac: A Biography*, New York: Paragon House, 1990.
Cook, Bruce. *The Beat Generation*, New York: Charles Scribner's Sons, 1971.
Coolidge, Clark. 'Kerouac', *The American Poetry Review*, Vol. 24, Jan./Feb. 1995, pp.43-49.
Creeley, Robert. 'Thinking of Jack: A Preface', in Jack Kerouac, Good Blonde and Others, Donald Allen, ed., revised ed., Grey Fox Press: 1993, pp. vii-xiii.
Dagier, Patricia and Hervé Quéméner. *Jack Kerouac: Au Bout de la Route ... La Bretagne*, Paris: An Here Publications, 1999.
Davidson, Michael. The San Francisco Renaissance: Poetics and Community at Mid-Century, Cambridge: Cambridge University Press, 1979.
Donaldson, Scott, ed., On the Road: Text and Criticism, New York: Penguin Books, 1979.
Dostoyevsky, Fyodor. Notes from the Underground and Other Stories, trans. Andrew R. MacAndrew, New York: Signet, 1961.

Eburne, Jonathan Paul. 'Trafficking in the Void: Burroughs, Kerouac and the Consumption of Otherness', Modern Fiction Studies, Vol. 43 No. 1, Spring 1997, pp.53-92.

Ellis, R. J. *Liar, Liar!—Jack Kerouac, Novelist*, London: Greenwich Exchange, 1999.

Férland, Remi, ed. 'Jack Kérouac au/on *Sel de la Semaine* (Radio-Canada, Montreal, 1967), *Les Avant-Dire de la Rencontre Internationale Jack Kérouac*, Quebec: Le Secrétariat permanent des peuples francophones, Septembre, 1987.

Feied. Frederick. *No Pie in the Sky: The Hobo as American Cultural Hero in the Works of Jack London, John Dos Passos and Jack Kerouac*, New York: Citadel Press, 1964.

French, Warren. *Jack Kerouac*, Boston: G. K. Hall, 1986.

Gelfant, Blanche H. 'Jack Kerouac', *Contemporary Literature* Vol. 15 No. 3, Summer 1974, pp.415-422.

Gifford, Barry and Lee, Lawrence. *Jack's Book: Jack Kerouac in the Lives and Words of His Friends,* London: Hamish Hamilton, 1979.

Ginsberg, Allen. *Journals Early Fifties Early Sixties*, New York: Grove Press, 1977.

Ginsberg, Allen. [Review of *Dharma Bums*], *Village Voice*, 12 November, 1958, pp.3-5.

Gussow, Alan. 'Bohemia Revisited: Malcolm Cowley, Jack Kerouac and *On the Road*', *Georgia Review*, Vol. 38, Summer 1984, pp.291-311.

Hamon, E., S.J., Les Canadiens-Français de la Nouvelle-Angleterre, Quebec; N. S. Hardy, 1891.

Haverty Kerouac, Joan (2000) *Nobody's Wife: the Smart Aleck and the King of the Beats*. New York: Creative Arts Books, 2000

Heubel, Harry Russell. *Jack Kerouac*, Boise: Boise State University Press, 1979

Holmes, John Clellon. *Nothing More to Declare*, London: Andre Deutsch, 1968.

Holmes, John Clellon Holmes, *Remembering Jack Kerouac*, Coventry: The Beat Scene Press, 2008

Holton, Robert. 'Kerouac Among the Fellahin; *On the Road* to the Postmodern', *Modern Fiction Studies*, Vol. 14 No. 2, pp.265-283.

Hipkiss, Robert A. *Jack Kerouac: Prophet of the New Romanticism*, Lawrence; The Regent's Press, 1976.

Hunt, Timothy. *Kerouac's Crooked Road*. Hamden, Conn.: Archon Books, 1981.

Jackson, Carl T. 'The counterculture looks East: beat writers and Asian religion', *American Studies*, Vol. 29, Spring 1988, pp.51-70.

Jarvis, Charles E. *Visions of Kerouac: The Life of Jack Kerouac*, New York: Ithaca Press, 1974.

Johnson, Ronna C. '"You're putting me on": Jack Kerouac and the Postmoldern Emergence', *College Literature* Vol. 27 No. 1 (Winter 2000), pp.22-38.

Jones, Leroi (Amiri Baraka) 'Letter to the Editors', *Evergreen Review* Vol. 2 No. 8 (Spring 1959), pp.254-5.

Joyce, James. *A Portrait of the Artist as a Young Man*, 1914-1915, rpt. Harmondsworth: Penguin, 1992.

Joyce, James. *Finnegans Wake*, 1934, rpt. London: Fáber and Faber, 1977.

Joyce, James. *Ulysses*, 1922, rpt. Harmondsworth: Penguin, 1968.

Kinsey, Alfred C. et. al., *Sexual Behavior in the Human Male*, Philadelphia: W. B. Saunders, 1948.

Lee, A. Robert Lee, ed., *The Beat Generation Writers*, London: Pluto Press, 1986.

Leed, Jacob. 'Gary Snyder, Han Shan and Jack Kerouac', *Journal of Modern Literature*, Vol. 11, March, pp.185-193.

Linick, Anthony. 'A History of the American Literary Avant-Garde', Ph.D. dissertation, University of California, Los Angeles, 1965.

McBride, Dick. 'Shouting Down the Line', *The Beat Journal*, Vol. 1 (1995), pp.86-90.

McClure, Michael. 'Jack's *Old Angel Midnight*', in *Old Angel Midnight*, San Francisco: Grey Fox Press, 1995, pp.xiii-xxi.

McNally, Dennis. *Desolate Angel: Jack Kerouac, the Beat Generation and America*, New York: McGraw Hill, 1979.

McNeil, Helen. 'The Archaeology of Gender in the Beat Movement', A. Robert Lee, ed., *The Beat Generation Writers*, London: Pluto Press, 1998, pp.178-199.

Maher, Jr., Paul M. *Empty Phantoms: Interviews and Encounters with Jack Kerouac*, New York: Thunder's Mouth Press, 2005

Maher, Jr., Paul M. *Kerouac: The Definitive Biography*. London : Taylor Trade Publishing, 2004.

Mailer, Norman. 'The White Negro', *Dissent*, Summer, 1953, pp.276-93.

Milewski, Robert J. *Jack Kerouac: An Annotated Bibliography of Secondary Sources, 1944-1979*, Metuchen, N.J.: Scarecrow Press, 1981.

Millstein, Gilbert. 'Books of the Times', *New York Times* 5 September 1957.

Moore, Dave. '*On the Road*: The Scroll Revealed', *The Kerouac Connection*, No. 10, April 1986, pp.3-7.

Moore, Dave. 'The Breton Traveller: Jack Kerouac's Search for his Roots', *The Kerouac Rag* No. 32 (Spring 2001), pp.3-5.

Montgomery, John. 'Jack Kerouac and the San Francisco Renaissance', 1974, unpublished typescript, The Nottingham Trent University Library.

Nicosia, Gerald. *Memory Babe*, 1983; rpt. Harmondsworth: Penguin, 1986.

Nicosia, Gerald. *The Two Lowells of Jack Kerouac*, 1988; rpt. Coventry: Beat Scene Press, 1993.

Panish, Jon. 'Kerouac's *The Subterraneans*: A Study of "Romantic Primitivism"', *MELUS*, Vol. 19 No. 3, Fall 1994, pp.107-123.

Parker, Brad. *Kerouac: An Introduction*, Lowell: Lowell Corporation for the Humanities, 1989.

Parkinson, Thomas. *A Casebook on the Beat*, New York: Thomas Y. Crowell, 1961.

Proust, Marcel *Remembrance of Things Past*, 3 vols., trans. C. K. Moncrieff and Terence Kilmartin, Harmondsworth: Penguin, 1981.

Rimbaud, Arthur. *Collected Poems*, trans. Oliver Bernard, Harmondsworth: Penguin, 1962.

Rosenberg, Rosalind. *Divided Lives: American Women in the Twentieth Century*. New York: Hill and Wang, 1992.

Spengler, Oswald, *The Decline of the West*, 1918-1922, rpt., trans. Charles Francis Atkinson, New York: Alfred A. Knopf, 1926.

Stimpson, Catherine R. 'The Beat Generation and the Trials of Homosexual Liberation', *Salmagundi* Vol. 58-59, 1982-83, pp.373-392

Tallman, Warren. 'Kerouac's Sound', 1959, rpt. in *Evergreen Review*, Vol.4 No.11, Jan.-Feb. 1960, pp.153-169.

Thoreau, Henry David. *A Week on the Concord and Merrimack Rivers*, 1849, rpt. in *Walden, A Week on the Concord and Merrimack Rivers*, Viking Press, 1947.

Turner, Steve. *Angelheaded Hipster: A Life of Jack Kerouac*, London: Bloomsbury, 1996.

Tytell, John. *Naked Angels: the lives and literature of the Beat Generation*, New York: McGraw Hill, 1976.

Van der Bent, Jaap. 'A French American: Kerouac's Double Identity', in Pierre Anctil, et. al, eds., *Un Homme Grand: Jack Kerouac at the Crossroads of Many Cultures*, Ottawa: Carleton, 1990, pp.195-200.

Vopat, Caroline Gottlieb. 'Jack Kerouac's On the Road: A Re-evaluation', *Midwest Quarterly*, Summer, 1973, pp.385-407.

Weinreich, Regina. *The Spontaneous Poetics of Jack Kerouac*, Carbondale: Southern Illinois University Press, 1987.

Widmer, Kingsley. 'The American Road', *University of Kansas City Review*, Vol. 26 No. 4, Summer 1960, pp.309-17.

Williams, William Carlos. *The Collected Early Poems*, London: MacGibbon and Key, 1951

Wolfe, Thomas. *Look Homeward, Angel*, 1929, rpt. London: New English Library, 1968.

Wolfe, Thomas. *Of Time and the River*, 1935, rpt. Harmondsworth: Penguin, 1971.

Permissions and Acknowledgements:

US postal service: Kerouac commemorative stamp.

Allen Ginsberg Estate and Peter Hale: Allen Ginsberg, Photograph of Jack Kerouac, 'East 7th Street at Ave A', New York, Fall 1953.

Allen Ginsberg Estate and Peter Hale: Allen Ginsberg, Photograph of Jack Kerouac, 'Probably 104 E 5 Street ... 1964 Fall'.

Christopher Gray for the pen and ink drawing of Jack Kerouac.